Magazine Advertising Graphics

P·I·E BOOKS

Magazine Advertising Graphics

Copyright©1998 by P · I · E BOOKS

All rights reserved. No part of this publication may be reproduced in any form or by any means, graphic, electronic or mechanical, including photocopying and recording by an information storage and retrieval system, without permission in writing from the publisher.

P · I · E BOOKS
Villa Phoenix Suite 301, 4-14-6, Komagome, Toshima-ku, Tokyo 170-0003 Japan
Tel: 03-3940-8302 Fax: 03-3576-7361
E-mail: piebooks@bekkoame.ne.jp

First Published and Distributed by:
Nippon Shuppan Hanbai Deutschland GmbH
Krefelder Str. 85, D-40549 Düsseldorf, Germany
Tel: (0211) 5048080 Fax: (0211) 5049326

I S B N 4 - 8 9 4 4 4 - 0 8 2 - 2

Printed in Japan

contents

004 intro

Steve Williams
Jon Matthews

広告には、はっとさせられる瞬間がある。
目をおおうような現実社会であったり、ありえないシチュエーションであったり、はたまた憧れていた世界の実現であったり……。
クリエイターの鋭い感覚と豊かな発想は、既成概念をうちこわし消費者に新たな価値観を与える。ここに紹介する１９ケ国より集められた作品は、パラパラめくる雑誌の中で、思わず手を止めてしまうインパクトと説得力を兼ね備えた秀作ばかりである。クリエイターの戦略、そして発想の源を探るべく、気になる２名のクリエイターに雑誌広告について彼等の考えを聞いてみた。しかしまたもやあっと言わされてしまったが……

Steve Williams
カール・マルクスが、かつて私に言った。
「スティーブ、ぼくがこう言っても怒らないでくれ。でも、広告屋ってやつらは、腐りかけた資本主義の残骸をえさにしている、うじ虫のようなやつらだな。」
言い終わると、彼はヴォッカを一気にあおった。私はそんな彼を見返した。気を悪くしたのではない。カールはよく、こんなことを持ち出しては、私を困らせようとしていた。
「ああ、きっと君が正しいんだろう、カール。ぼくらはおそらく、むさぼり食うために、かわいそうな宿主を待ちつづけている寄生虫以外の何者でもない。だが、ぼくらは情報の提供者でもあるんだ。プロレタリアートに対して自由に知識を与えているのさ。そうしてやらなければ、彼らは無知のまま世界から取り残されてしまうかもしれないからね。」
「どっちなんだい？」カールはおもしろそうにたずねた。
「ああ、友よ。どっちかだって？だれが気にするものか。君以外ね。しかも君はもう死んでいるんだぜ。」
カールは、分け合って飲んでいたヴォッカのボトルをひょいと取り上げた。
「君がそんなふうな態度なら、顔も見たくないね。」
そう言い放つと、彼は部屋を出ていった。

プロフィール
Steve Williamsは、ロンドンのLowe Howard-Spinkをベースに活動して８年になる（たぶん、そこ以外では仕事がないからだ）。そして、まる１日、ライターのAdrian Limとコンピューターゲームに興じている。Steve は、実は「マラソン」が得意である。ところが、Adrianはまったくダメだ。死ぬ気で頑張れない。残念なことである。なぜなら、最後まで生き残ることがこのゲームの目的なのだから。

John Matthews
雑誌広告は、記事よりもおもしろくあるべきではないだろうか。でなければ、だれが広告など読むものか。編集者は読者に攻撃的な広告を却下するべきか。いや、それよりも退屈な広告を拒否するべきでは。あらゆる雑誌広告が、読者からのダイレクトな反応を呼ぶものでなければならないとしたら。もし、クーポンに「この広告が好きです。はい・いいえ」といった質問があったら。もし、だれもそれに答えようとしなかったら。将来の雑誌は、10％がリサイクルペーパーで、90％がリサイクル広告になるのか。２冊の雑誌に同じ記事が載っていたら、両方とも読むか。

プロフィール
Jon Matthewsは、アムステルダムのWieden & Kennedyのクリエイティブ・ディレクターである。彼の持論は、「広告らしくない広告ほど、クライアントにとっては良いものとなる」である。

intro

Advertisements can often be startling.
They might depict one of the realities of society that people would rather pretend not exist; completely fanciful situations; or the realization of a world that you long to see.
Designers, armed with keen sensibilities and rich imaginations, attempt to destroy currently held concepts while presenting new values to the consumer.
Collected from 19 countries, the advertisements presented here all have the ability to bring a reader's hand to a screeching halt as it flips casually through a magazine, such is the impact and persuasive power of these outstanding works.
To better understand creative strategies, and to explore the sources of imagination, we asked two talented designers for their views on magazine advertising. Even their comments turn out to be startling...

Steve Williams
Karl Marx once said to me, "Steve, don't be offended when I say this, but I've often thought that Advertisers are maggots feeding on the rotting corpse of capitalism." I looked at him as he knocked back his vodka, I wasn't offended, he often came out with shit like that just to wind me up. "Perhaps you're right Karl. Perhaps we are nothing more than parasites, waiting for an unsuspecting host to gorge ourselves on. On the other hand, perhaps we are the givers of information. Freely imparting knowledge to the proleteriat, who might otherwise remain ignorant to the world around them." "Which is it?" He asked intrigued. "Ahh, my friend," I replied. "Who knows? Who cares? Except you, and you're dead." Karl picked up the bottle of vodka we'd been sharing. "If you're going to be like that you can piss off," he said. And left the room.

PROFILE:
Steve Williams works at Lowe Howard-Spink, London. He's been there eight years (probably because he can't get a job anywhere else) and spends his days playing computer games with his writer, Adrian Lim. Steve is actually very good at "Marathon," whereas Adrian can't play to save his life. Which is a shame, because that's the object of the game.

John Matthews
Shouldn't the advertising in a magazine be more interesting than the editorial? If it isn't, why would anyone bother reading it? Should an editor turn down ads that might offend his readers, or should he turn down ads that might bore them? What if all magazine ads had to be direct response? What if the coupon read: "I liked your ad - YES/NO" ? What if no-one could be bothered to reply? Will the magazine of the future be 10% recycled woodpulp, 90% recycled ads? If you saw the same article in two magazines, how many of them would you read?

PROFILE:
Jon Matthews is a creative director at Wieden & Kennedy in Amsterdam. He subscribes to the view that the less the work the agency produces looks or sounds like advertising, the better the job it is doing for the clients.

duction

Anzeigen lassen uns oft erstaunen. Sie mögen eine der gesellschaftlichen Realitäten abbilden, von denen die Leute lieber sagen würden, sie existierten nicht; komplett kuriose Situationen; oder die Realisation einer Wunschwelt. Designer, gerüstet mit kühner Sensibilität und reicher Vorstellungskraft, bemühen sich, jetzt noch gültige Konzepte zu zerstören und gleichzeitig den Konsumenten neue Werte zu präsentieren. Zusammengetragen aus 19 Ländern, haben alle hier präsentierten Anzeigen die Fähigkeit, die Hand des Lesers beim lockeren Blättern durch eine Zeitschrift zum apprupten Halt zu bringen-so stark ist der spontane Eindruck und die Überzeugungskraft dieser außergewöhnlichen Arbeiten. Um die kreativen Strategien besser zu verstehen und die Quellen der Imagination zu erforschen, haben wir zwei talentierte Designer um ihre Ansichten über Zeitschriftenanzeigen gebeten. Selbst ihre Kommentare erweisen sich als verblüffend...

Steve Williams

Karl Marx sagte einmal zu mir: „Steve, sei nicht verletzt, wenn ich das sage, aber ich habe oft gedacht, daß Werbeleute Maden sind, die sich vorn verrottenden Körper des Kapitalismus ernahren." Ich schaute ihn an. wie er seinen Wodka hinunterkippte, ich war nicht verletzt, er kam oft mit solchem Mist, nur um mich aufzuziehen. „Vielleicht hast Du recht, Karl. Vielleicht sind wir nichts anderes als Parasiten, die auf einen unerwarteten Wirt warten, um sich in ihn einzugraben. Andererseits sind wir möglicherweise Vermittler von Informationen. Grosszügig Wissen an das Proletariat vermittelnd, das andernfalls ignorant gegenüber der es umgebenden Welt bleibt." „Was ist es?", fragte er verwirrt. „Ann, mein Freund", entgegnete ich. „Wer weiss? Wer Kümmert sich? Ausser Dir, und Du bist tot." Karl ergriff die Wodkaflasche, die wir geteilt hatten. „Wenn Du weiter so bist, kannst Du abhauen", sagte er. Und verliess den Raum.

PROFIL:
Steve Williams arbeitet bei Lowe Howard-Spink, London. Er ist dort seit acht Jahren (wahrscheinlich, weil er nirgends sonst einen Job bekommen kann) und verbringt den Tag mit Computerspielen gemeinsam mit seinem Texter Adrian Lim. Steve ist besonders gut in „Marathon", wohingegen Adrian es beim Spielen nicht schafft, sein Leben zu retten. Was schade ist, weil gerade das das Ziel des Spiels ist.

John Matthews

Sollte die Werbung in einer Zeitschrift interessanter sein als die redaktionellen Beiträge? Wenn dem nicht so ist, warum sollte dann jemand sie lesen wollen? Sollte ein Herausgeber Anzeigen ablehnen, die seine Leser verletzen könnten, oder sollte er Anzeigen ablehnen, die langweilen könnten? Was, wenn alle Anzeigen Reaktionsanzeigen sein müssten? Was, wenn auf dem Coupon stünde: „Ich fand ihre Anzeiga gut - JA/NEIN"? Was, wenn niemand veranlasst werden könnte, zu antworten? Wird die Zeitschrift der Zukunft zu 10% aus Recycling-Zellstoff und zu 90% aus Recycling-Anzeigen bestehen? Wenn Sie den gleichen Artikel in zwei Zeitschriften sehen würden, wie viele davon würden Sie lesen?

PROFIL:
Jon Matthes ist der Creative Director bei Wieden & Kennedy in Amsterdam. Er vertritt die Ansicht, je weniger die Arbeit einer Werbeagentur aussehe oder klinge wie Werbung, umso besser werde die Aufgabe für den Kunden erfüllt.

Editorial Notes
Credit Format
Client
Type of Company
Country from which submitted / Year of completion

CD: Creative Director

AD: Art Director

D: Designer

P: Photographer

I: Illustrator

CW: Copywriter

PD: Producer

DF: Design Firm

A: Advertising Agency

Magazine
Advertising
Graphics

Philips New Zealand
Audio Equipment Manufacturer
オーディオ機器製造販売
New Zealand 1997
CD, AD, D: Dave Bolton
P: Shaun Pettigrew
CW: Andrew Ayers
A: Walkers Advertising

We do incredible things with sound.
音の不可能を可能にする

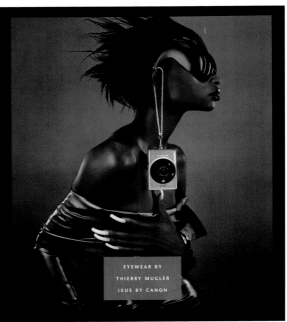

Canon Europa N.V.
Camera Manufacturer 精密機器製造販売
Netherlands 1997
CD, AD: Rob Sikkink
AD: Tom Fincham (3,4)
P: Jean-Baptist Mondino (1,2) / Jerome Esch (3,4)
CW: Paul McManus
Styling: Ruud van der Peijl (1,2) / Elle Hagen (3,4)
Artbuying: Nicole Nijsen
A: TBWA / H Neth-Work B. V.

1: Make up by M.A.C. IXUS L-1 by Canon
　メイク・アップはM.A.C.、IXUS L-1はキャノン
2: Eyewear by Thierry Mugler IXUS by Canon
　サングラスはThierry Mugler、IXUSはキャノン
3: Dress by DKNY IXUS by Canon
　ドレスはDKNY、IXUSはキャノン。
4: Sneakers by VANS IXUS L-1 by Canon
　スニーカーはVANS、IXUS L-1はキャノン

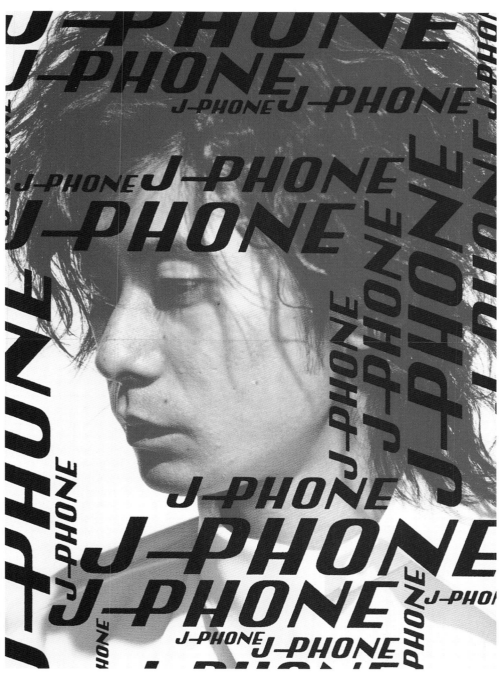

Tokyo Digital Phone
Cellular Phone Company
携帯電話会社
Japan 1997
CD: Yasumichi Oka
AD, D: Kazunari Hattori
P: Takeshi Kano
A: Light Publicity Ltd./ Dentsu Inc.

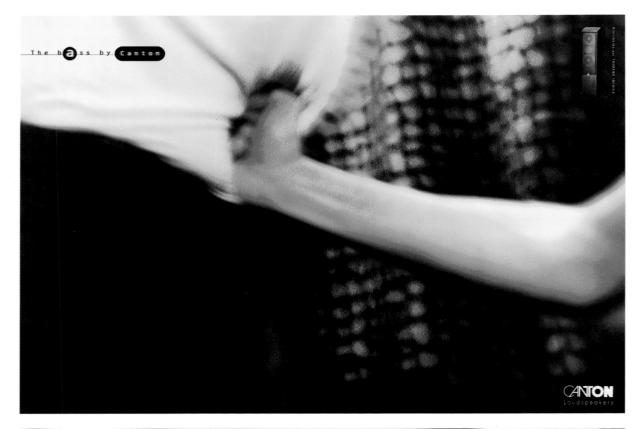

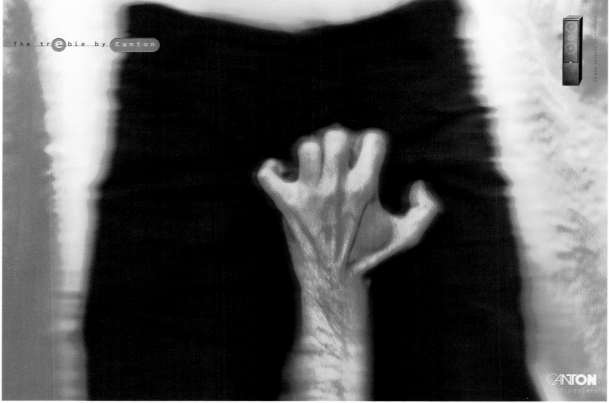

Thorens
Audio Equipment Manufacturer
オーディオ機器製造販売
Spain 1997
CD: Victor Curto
AD: Manuel Padilla
P: Miguel Angel Nalda
CW: Carles Grau
A: Tiempo / BBDO

1: バスはキャントン。
   The bass by Canton
2: トレブルはキャントン。
   The treble by Canton

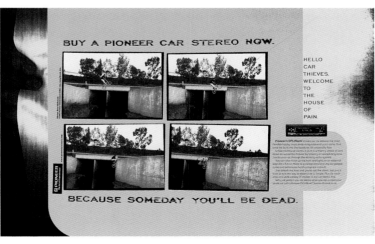

1
2 3
4

1: I am a king with a bucket
seat for a throne. Friends
receive the bounty of my
kingdom. Thieves receive
painful bleeding eardrums.
俺が王様だ。バケットシートは俺
のもんだ。仲間には最高の気分を
味わせてやる。盗むヤツは耳から
血でも流してろ。

Pioneer Electronics
Audio Equipment Manufacturer
オーディオ機器製造販売
USA 1997
Chief Creative Officer: David Lubars
CD: Dante Lombardi
AD: Rohitash Rao
P: Tom Nelson（1）
/ Scott Serfas（main image）（2）
/ Whitey McConnaughy（sequence image）（2）
/ Lance Dawes（main shot）（3）
/ Grant Brittain（sub-visuals）（3）
/ Brad McDonald（4）
A: BBDO West

Sony Corp.
Electric Equipment Manufacturer
電気製品製造販売
Japan 1998
CD: Toshiro Fumizono
AD, D: Yutaka Murakoshi
P: Taka Kobayashi
CW: Kotaro Shimada

New earstyle
初耳スタイル
1: Even when your hair's perfect, you can still have music.
きれいに髪を結った日も、音楽を休まない。

2: Hair ornaments are important. So is music.
　髪飾りも大事。音楽も大事。
3: I had given up on headphones
　ヘッドホンなんて、アタマからあきらめていた。
4: A lady just doesn't go out if her hair is a mess.
　レディは髪がくずれたら、もう出かけません。

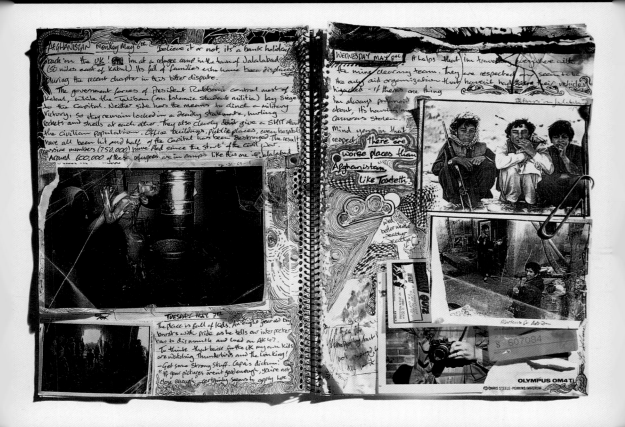

LA Cellular
Cellular Phone Company 携帯電話会社
USA 1996
Chief Creative Officer: David Lubars
CD: Chris Robb
Writer: Harold Einstein
CW: Kathy Hepinstall
P: Geoff Adler
A: BBDO West

This word lost during a cell phone conversation on 3/7/96.
96年3月7日 セルラー電話での会話中に迷子になった言葉です。

Olympus Optical Co., Ltd.
Camera Manufacturer
精密機器製造販売
UK 1996
CD: Paul Weinberger
AD: Brian Campbell
P: David Bailey
CW: Ben Priest
A: Lowe Howard-Spink

1: What's your favourite smell? A Sunday roast in the oven, your wife's perfume, or is it a dead heat between
    developer and acid stop bath?
    好きな匂いは？日曜日のオーブンのローストビーフや奥さんの香水の匂い。それとも現像液と酸性停止浴液の合わさったにおい？
2: I have this recurring dream: me, Kate Moss and a huge tub of ilford HP420 1600 ASA.
    夢をよく見るよ。俺とケート・モスとイルフォード HP420 1600 ASA のでっかいタブの夢だ。

Airborne Early Warning and Control.
空中からの早期警戒と誘導管制
The right technologies. Right now.
暮らしを守る先端技術がここに
It's easier to get out of harm's way when you can see it coming from hundreds of miles away.
発見さえ早ければ、どんな攻撃も簡単に回避できます。

Northrop Grumman
Aerospace Company　航空機製造販売
USA　1997
CD: David Lubars
AD: Rob Palmer
CW: Max Godsil / Steve Hayden
I: How Studio
Photography: FPG
A: BBDO West

Slik blir fruktene dine hvis du oppbevarer dem lenge i et vanlig kjøleskap.

Slik blir fruktene dine hvis du oppbevarer dem lenge i et kjøleskap fra Zanussi.

For at frukt og grønnsaker ikke skal tørke ut, må de ha riktig luftfuktighet. Derfor har vi utviklet Crisp'n Fresh. Dette oppbevaringssystemet bevarer formen og smaken på fruktene dine bedre enn i et vanlig kjøleskap. Besøker du nærmeste AKA-butikk eller Zanussi-forhandler, kan du vinne et Crisp'n Fresh-kjøleskap.

ZANUSSI

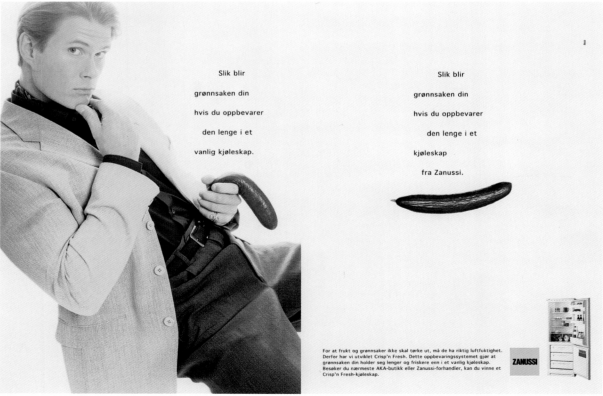

Slik blir grønnsaken din hvis du oppbevarer den lenge i et vanlig kjøleskap.

Slik blir grønnsaken din hvis du oppbevarer den lenge i et kjøleskap fra Zanussi.

For at frukt og grønnsaker ikke skal tørke ut, må de ha riktig luftfuktighet. Derfor har vi utviklet Crisp'n Fresh. Dette oppbevaringssystemet gjør at grønnsaken din holder seg lenger og friskere enn i et vanlig kjøleskap. Besøker du nærmeste AKA-butikk eller Zanussi-forhandler, kan du vinne et Crisp'n Fresh-kjøleskap.

ZANUSSI

1
2

Zanussi
Electric Equipment Manufacturer
電気製品製造販売
Norway 1998
AD: Øivind Lie
P: Johan Wildhagen
CW: Ragnar Roksvåg
A: Bold Reklamebyrå As

1: If a fruit has been kept in an ordinary refrigerator, it becomes like this.
　 If a fruit has been kept in a Zanussi refrigerator, it becomes like this even after a long time.
　 フルーツは、普通の冷蔵庫に長く入れておくとこのようになる。
　 Zanussiの冷蔵庫ならば、長く入れておいてもこのとおり。
2: If a vegetable has been kept in an ordinary refrigerator, it becomes like this.
　 If a vegetable has been kept in a Zanussi refrigerator, it becomes like this even after a long time.
　 普通の冷蔵庫は、野菜を長く入れておくとこのようになる。
　 Zanussiの冷蔵庫ならば、野菜を長く入れておいてもこのとおり。

1: If a tomato is to be thrown at someone, choose a fresh one as much as possible.
人に投げつけるトマトならば、できるだけ新鮮なものを
2: A shriveled carrot can get nobody hooked.
萎びたニンジンでは、だれもひっかけられない。
3: A decayed apple can attract nobody.
腐ったリンゴでは、人を誘惑することはできない。

Zanussi
Electric Equipment Manufacturer
電気製品製造販売
Norway 1998
AD: Stephanie Dumont
P: Espen Tollefsen
CW: Ragnar Roksvåg
A: Bold Reklamebyrå As

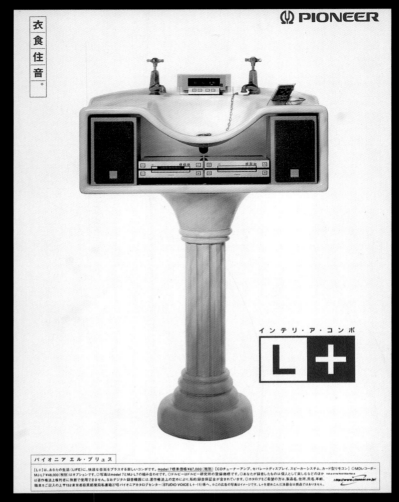

Pioneer Electronic Corp.
Audio Equipment Manufacturer
オーディオ機器製造販売
Japan 1997
CD: Tetsuya Sakota
AD: Hideaki Masuda
D: Nobuo Omichi
P: Kazunari Koyama
CW: Hiroshi Hasegawa
Art: Masato Okamura
A: Asatsu Inc.

Food. Clothing. Shelter. Music.
衣・食・住・音。

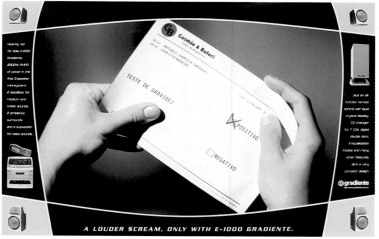

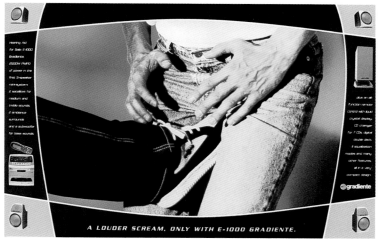

1
2 3
4 5

1: Gradiente energy. 2500w have never been as compact.
グラディエンテ・エネルギー2500w。こんなにコンパクトなものがあったでしょうか
2,3,5: A louder scream. Only with E-1000 Gradiente.
もっと大きい金切り声が出せるのは、E-1000グラディエンテだけ。
4: Gradiente energy 2500w
グラディエンテ・エネルギー2500w

Gradiente
Electric Equipment Manufacturer
電気製品製造販売
Brazil 1997
CD: Alexandre Gama
AD: Rodrigo Butori
P: Fernando Zuffo (1) /
Klaus Mitteldorf (2,3,5) /
Cassio Vasconcelos (2,3,4,5,) /
Pedro Lobo (4)
CW: Gustavo Gusmão
A: Young & Rubicam Brasil

Gradiente
Electric Equipment Manufacturer
電気製品製造販売
Brazil 1997
CD: Alexandre Gama
AD: Rodrigo Butori
P: Cassio Vasconcelos
CW: Átila Francucci
A: Young & Rubicam Brasil

1: If you want power, you want Gradiente.
パワーが欲しいならグラディエンテ
2: What kind of system have you listened to lately?
最近、どんなステレオ聴いてますか
3: The neighbour upstairs has a Gradiente sound system.
上の階の住人はグラディエンテを持っている

Hollywood stars will take over your home.

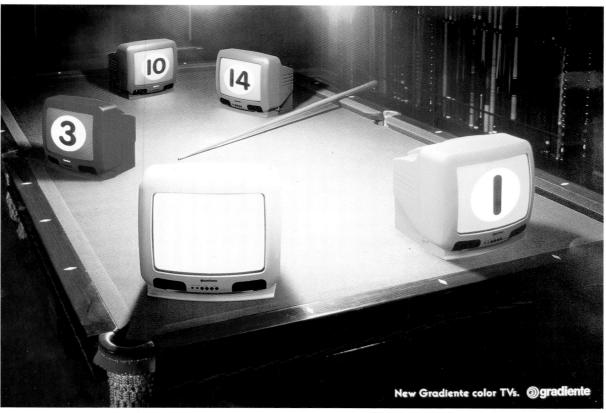

New Gradiente color TVs. gradiente

1: Hollywood stars will take over your home.
ハリウッドのスターがあなたのお宅を乗っ取ります

1: **Gradiente**
Electric Equipment Manufacturer
電気製品製造販売
Brazil 1997
CD: Alexandre Gama
AD: Rogerio Lima
P: Fernando Zuffo
CW: Átila Francucci
A: Young & Rubicam Brasil

2: **Gradiente**
Electric Equipment Manufacturer
電気製品製造販売
Brazil 1997
CD: Alexandre Gama
AD: Rodrigo Butori
P: Fernando Zuffo
CW: Gustavo Gusmão
A: Young & Rubicam Brasil

1
2

Horsepower is useless without 4x4 traction.
F-1000. The only 4x4 in the category.

You won't lose your car
in the parking lot anymore.

Ford Ka. The face of the new.

Ford
Auto Manufacturer
自動車製造販売
Brazil 1997
CD: Alexandre Gama
AD: Rogerio Lima (1) / Rodrigo Butori (2,3,4) / J R D'Elboux (2,3)
P: Mario Fontes (1) / Fernando Zuffo (2,3) / Hilton Ribeiro (3) / Willy Biondani (4)
CW: Atila Francucci (1) / Alexandre Gama (2,3) / Rita Corradi (2,3) / Gustavo Gusmão (2,3)
A: Young & Rubicam Brasil

1: Horsepower is useless without 4 X 4 traction.
　４×４の牽引力がなければ馬力も無意味
2: You won't lose your car in the parking lot anymore.
　駐車場で車をなくすことは、もうないでしょう
3: We know exactly what you have in mind
　私たちはあなたが欲しいものを、知っています
4: Ford Ka. The face of the new
　フォード車。新しさの顔。

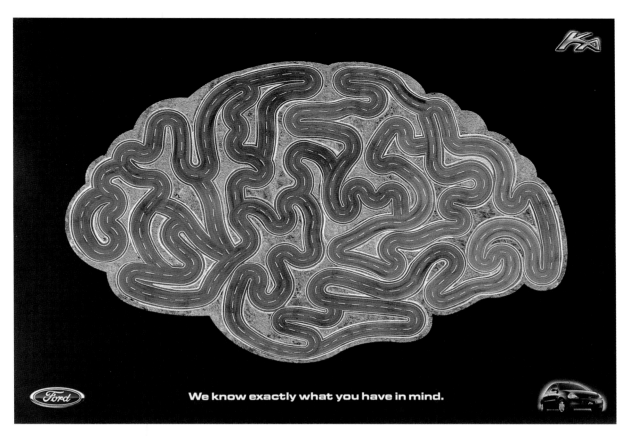

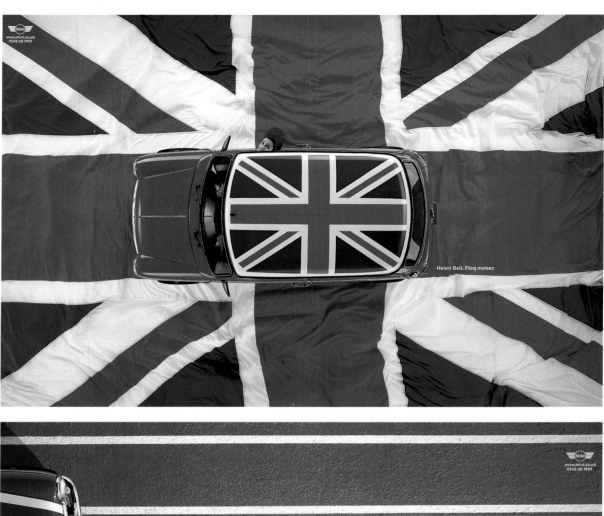

Rover
Auto Manufacturer 自動車製造販売
UK 1997
CD: Nik Welch
AD: Melanie Forster
P: Frank Herholdt
CW: Michelle Stewart
A: Ammirati Puris Lintas

1: Helen Bell. Flag Maker. / ヘレン・ベル。国旗屋。
2: Mick Oxberry. Athlete. / ミック・オクスベリ。アスリート
3: Paul Watts. Tiler. / ポール・ワッツ。タイル屋。
4: John Hine. Composer. / ジョン・ハイン。作曲家。

Weltweit spielen über 40 Millionen Kinder Fußball.

Der Bremsassistent BAS. Eine Idee aus der S-Klasse.

▶ Kinder strapazieren ihren Schutz-
engel oft bis zum äußersten. Ein Umstand,
der unsere Ingenieure jeden Tag von neuem

antreibt, Systeme zu entwickeln, die we-
sentlich zur Sicherheit im Straßenverkehr
beitragen. Wie z.B. die Weltneuheit B.A.S.

Das System erkennt blitzschnell, wenn
der Fahrer im Notfall zu schwach auf die
Bremse tritt. Und aktiviert dann sofort

zusätzliche Bremskraft. So verkürzt sich
der Bremsweg um bis zu 40 %. Das sind
bei 50 km/h immerhin ca. 11 Meter. Und

die können auf der Straße noch wichtiger
sein als auf dem Fußballplatz. Infos unter
Tel. 01 30/01 40 Fax 01 30/01 41

Mercedes-Benz

Weil Straßen nicht immer aus Asphalt sind.

Das elektronische Stabilitätsprogramm ESP. Eine Idee aus der S-Klasse.

▶ In Deutschland gibt es mehr Regen-
als Sonnentage. Eine Tatsache, die nicht nur
die Meteorologen beschäftigt, sondern auch

die besten Ingenieure zum Handeln zwang.
Ihr Ergebnis: das vollkommen neuartige
elektronische Stabilitätsprogramm ESP. In

Sekundenbruchteilen erkennt ESP, ob ein
Fahrzeug auszubrechen droht. Sofort bremst
es die einzelnen Räder unabhängig von-

einander ab, erhöht oder drosselt notfalls so-
gar die Motorleistung. Ein wichtiger Beitrag
zu mehr Sicherheit. Und eine Weltneuheit,

die eines Tages genauso in jedes erstklassige
Auto gehören wird wie ABS und Airbags.
Tel. 01 30/01 40 Fax 01 30/01 41

Mercedes-Benz

Mercedes-Benz
Auto Manufacturer 自動車製造販売
Germany 1997
CD: Kurt-Georg Dickert (Art) / Stefan Schmidt (Text)
AD, DF: Axel Thomsen (Art)
AD, CW: Alexander Schill
AD, CW: Alexander Jaggy (Text)
P: Thomas Herbich / George Kavanagh
D, CW, DF: Springer & Jacoby Advertising GmbH

1: More than 40 million kids around the world play soccer.
世界中で４千万以上の子供たちがサッカーをしている。
2: Because not all roads are paved with asphalt.
なぜなら、全ての道路がアスファルト舗装されているわけではないから。

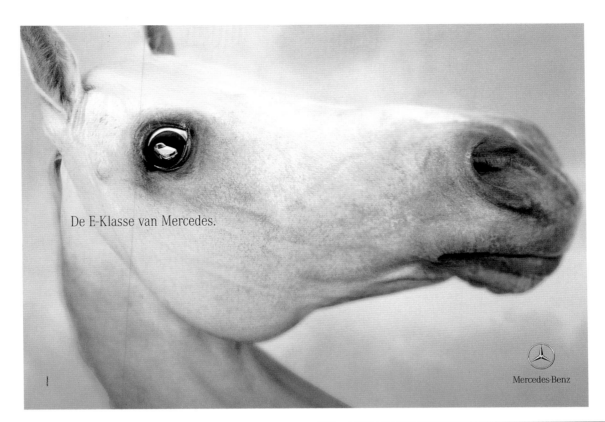

Mercedes-Benz
Auto Manufacturer
自動車製造販売
Belgium 1998
CD, AD: Werner Van Reck
AD: Paul Popelier
P: Christophe Gilbert
A: Ldv / Partners

LIFE IS LONG STRETCHES OF WORK SEPARATED BY BURSTS OF REWARDS. Shouldn't there be a reward at the end of the day? Something that makes you feel at home the moment you slip behind the wheel? You see, the BMW 7 Series isn't a car you drive to impress others. But to impress yourself it has the ability to connect with you. Listen to you. Respond to you. And reward you. With every turn of the wheel

WHY DO SO MANY INSIST ON PUTTING IT ON A PEDESTAL? The worldwide press has bestowed nearly every accolade on the BMW 7 Series. It is undeniably powerful, luxurious and spacious. Yet even a short stint behind the wheel reveals that it transcends mere features and statistics. It is invigorating, involving, thrilling. Making it more than a possession, but rather an obsession.

あなたを動かす、これまでなかったボルボです。

New **Volvo C70 coupe** 動かない姿にもパワーがあります。 **VOLVO**

0120-55-8500 http://www.volvocars.co.jp

1 2
3

1,2: **BMW**   3: **Volvo Cars Japan Corp.**
Auto Manufacturer 自動車製造販売   Auto Importer
USA 1997   自動車輸入販売
CD: Bruee Bildsten   Japan 1998
AD: Dean Hanson
P: Rodney Smith
CW: Tom Rosen
A: Fallon McElligott

1: Life is long stretches of work separated by bursts of rewards.
人はつかの間の充足感のために働き続けているのです。
2: Why do so many insist on putting it on a pedestal?
なぜこれほどまでに崇拝されるのでしょう？
3: An unprecedented Volvo moves your mind.
あなたを動かす。これまでなかったボルボです。

The Knowledge. Now available on the Audi A8.

The A8 now comes with its own taxi driver, better known as the Audi Navigation System. It guides the car using signals from satellites orbiting the earth. Just like a cabbie, it will whisk you to your destination by the most appropriate route. Unlike a cabbie, it will only talk to you when absolutely necessary.

Audi ⊙⊙⊙⊙
Vorsprung durch Technik

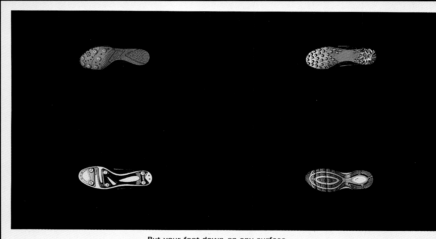

Put your foot down on any surface.

Nothing grips the road like an Audi quattro. The permanent four wheel drive system monitors each wheel independently and distributes the power when and where you need it most. Which means a sure footing, whatever the conditions.

Audi ⊙⊙⊙⊙
Vorsprung durch Technik

Can we race now?

Audi's quattro technology is so superior it's been banned worldwide from the 1998 Touring Car Championships. To even things up perhaps we should race something with three wheel drive. Ernie the Milkman is on standby.

Audi ⊙⊙⊙⊙
Vorsprung durch Technik

1
2 3

1: The knowledge. Now available on the Audi A8.
道はアウディＡ８に聞け。
2: Can we race now?
これなら互角に戦えますか？
3: Put your foot down on any surface.
踏み込めない場所はない。

Audi
Auto Manufacturer　自動車製造販売
UK　1998
CD: John Hegarty
AD: Tony McTear
P, I: Jack Bankhead
CW: Jeremy Carr
Typographer: Andy Bird
A: Bartle Bogle Hegarty Ltd.

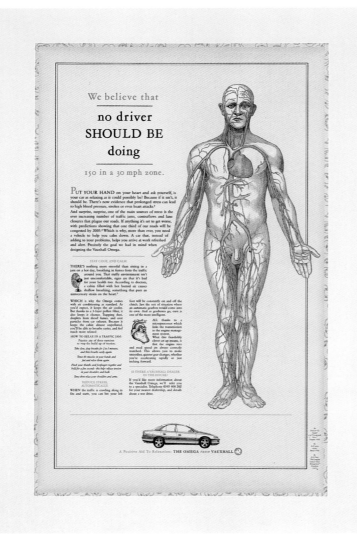

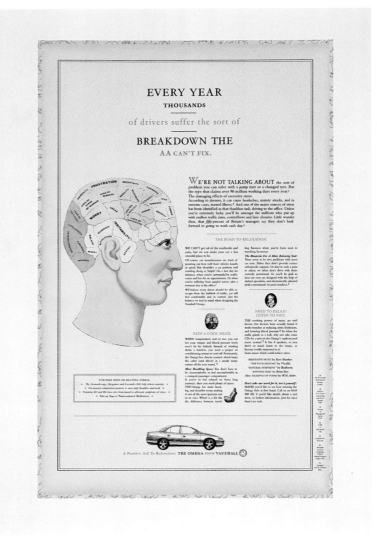

Vauxhall Motors
Auto Manufacturer 自動車製造販売
UK 1997
CD: Paul Weinberger
AD: Steve Williams
I: Bob Venables
CW: Adrian Lim
Typographer: Simon Warden
A: Lowe Howard-Spink

1: We believe that no driver should be doing 150 in a 30 mph zone.
制限速度30マイルの道で 150マイル出す人はいないはず。
2: Every year thousands of drivers suffer the sort of breakdown the AA can't fix.
毎年、何千というドライバーがＡＡでも直せない破損にみまわれます。
3: The warning signs that PRECEDE some heart attacks: "Delays ahead" " Road works" And "Contraflow".
発作に先立つ標識：「この先渋滞」「工事中」「片側通行」
4: New research shows that road rage kills millions every day.
最新の調査結果によれば、路上でのいら立ちがもとで毎日何百万人も死んでいるとか。

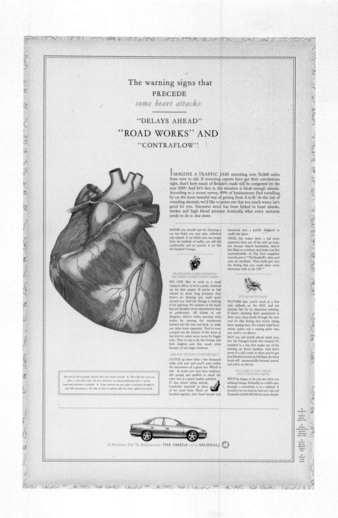

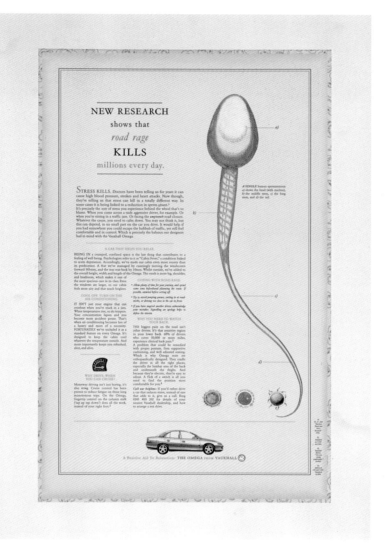

1: **Honda Motor Co., Ltd.**
Auto Manufacturer 自動車製造販売
Japan 1998
CD: Minoru Fujii
AD: Kashiwa Sato
D: Jun Kamata / Tadashi Yui
P: Takeshi Kano
CW: Satoshi Suzuki / Ken Inoue
A: Hakuhodo Inc.

2: **Volkswagen UK Ltd.**
Auto Manufacturer 自動車製造販売
UK 1996
CD: Tony Cox
AD: Jerry Hollens
Model Maker: Gavin Linsey
P: Mike Parsons
CW: Mike Boles
A: BMP DDB

1: Where can we go with the kids? / こどもといっしょにどこいこう。

メルセデス・ベンツ日本株式会社

もういちど、自動車を発明します。

世界で初めて自動車を発明した私たちが、つくらなければならない自動車がありました。

これからの自動車に、求められるものは何だろう。その答えの一つを探る時、私たちは矛盾した課題に直面しました。それは、都市の道路事情や省エネルギーを考慮したサイズでありながら、居住性や快適性、そしてメルセデスと呼ばれるのにふさわしい安全性を確保すること。しかし、従来の自動車づくりの常識では、この課題を解決できませんでした。道を開いたのは、"サンドイッチ・コンセプト"と

いう革新的アイデア(これからじっくりご説明していきます)。こうしたまったく新しい考え方の積み重ねが、まったく新しいメルセデス、Aクラスを生んだのです。昨日までの常識にとらわれず、今日からの常識をつくる。私たちの胸は高鳴っています。初めて自動車を発明した、あの日のように。

(The A-Class is coming.)

 Mercedes-Benz

A-ROOM Aクラスのコンセプトを紹介したパンフレットを差し上げます。☎0120-190-610 ●受付時間/月曜日〜金曜日 午前9時〜午後5時 ●土・日・祝日は除きます

ホームページでもAクラスを紹介しています。http://www.mbj.mercedes-benz.com

Once again, we invent the automobile.
もういちど、自動車を発明します。

Mercedes-Benz Japan Co., Ltd.
Auto Manufacturer 自動車製造販売
Japan 1997
CD: Takehiko Miura / Mitsuhiro Wada
AD: Kazumi Murata
D: Koichiro Toda / Jinya Nakamura / Masayuki Kobayashi
P: Kazuyasu Hagane
CW: Makoto Tsunoda / Sachiko Nishihashi
Creative coordinator: Manako Oshima
DF: Taki Corp.
A: Dentsu Inc.

Muß ein Gemälde aussehen wie ein Gemälde?

Muß eine Familie aussehen wie eine Familie?

Audi
Auto Manufacturer
自動車製造販売
Germany 1997
CD: Deneke von Weltzien
AD: Roland Schwarz
D: Nicole Hoefer
P: Uwe Duettmann
CW: Sebastian Hardieck / Timm Weber
A: JvM

1: Must a picture look like a picture? Must a saloon look like a saloon? The new Audi A6. Visions start with questions.
絵は絵のように見えなければならないのか？　リムジンはリムジンのように見えなければならないのか？　新しいアウディー6。ヴィジョンは問いかけから始まる。
2: Must a family look like a family? Must a saloon look like a saloon? The new Audi A6. Visions start with questions.
家族は家族のように見えなければならないのか？　リムジンはリムジンのように見えなければならないのか？　新しいアウディー6。ヴィジョンは問いかけから始まる。

Muß ein Philosoph aussehen wie ein Philosoph?

Muß eine Limousine aussehen wie eine Limousine?   Der neue Audi A6. Visionen beginnen mit Fragen.

Audi

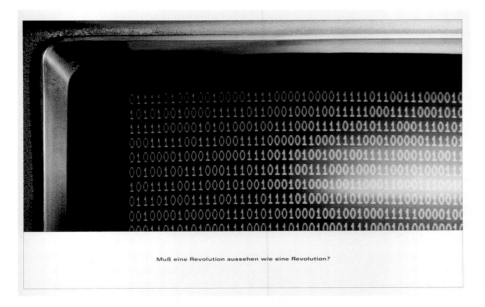

Muß eine Revolution aussehen wie eine Revolution?

Muß eine Limousine aussehen wie eine Limousine?   Der neue Audi A6. Visionen beginnen mit Fragen.

Audi

3
4

3: Must a philosopher look like a philosopher? Must a saloon look like a saloon? The new Audi A6. Visions start with questions.
哲学者は哲学者のように見えなければならないのか？　リムジンはリムジンのように見えなければならないのか？　新しいアウディー6。ヴィジョンは問いかけから始まる。
4: Must revolution look like a revolution? Must a saloon look like a saloon? The new Audi A6. Visions start with questions.
革命は革命のように見えなければならないのか？　リムジンはリムジンのように見えなければならないのか？　新しいアウディー6。ヴィジョンは問いかけから始まる。

Honda Motor Co., Ltd.
Auto Manufacturer 自動車製造販売
Japan 1996
CD: Minoru Fujii
AD: Kashiwa Sato
D: Jun Kamata / Akifumi Nishiura / Jun Oyamada
P: Takeshi Kano
CW: Satoshi Suzuki
A: Hakuhodo Inc.

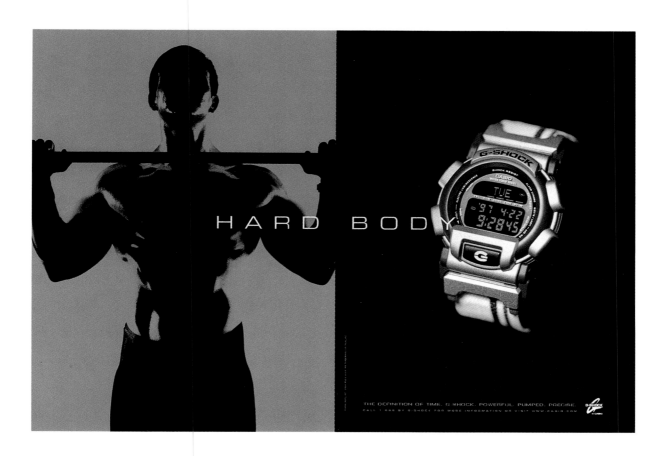

HARD BODY

THE DEFINITION OF TIME. G SHOCK. POWERFUL. PUMPED. PRECISE.
CALL 1 800 BY G-SHOCK FOR MORE INFORMATION OR VISIT WWW.CASIO.COM

CASIO

Slammin' The Rhythm
Groove Tune

G-SHOCK Baby-G
G'MIX   G'MIX

Get Tough.

CASIO

Revin' The Max.
Digital Tune

G-COOL
G'MIX

Get Tough. G-COOL

1,2,4,5: **Casio Computer Co., Ltd.**
Consumer Electronics Manufacturer & Sales
電子機器製造販売
Japan 1997
CD: Yasuhiko Shimura
AD: Keiichiro Fukushima
D: Akihiro Inou (1,2) / Makiko Adachi (4,5)
P: Taka Kobayashi (1) / Hiroshi Sato (Product) (1,4,5)
/ Kazunari Tajima (1,4,5) / Hiromasa Gamo (2)
CW: Akihiko Kawai / Jeffry Keeling
English Copy: Ventura Associates Inc.
DF: Geo Graphics Inc. (1,2)

3: **Casio, Inc.**
Consumer Electronics
Manufacturer & Sales
電子機器製造販売
USA 1997

Seiko Corp.
Watch Manufacturer 時計製造販売
Japan 1998
CD: Satoru Yokokawa
AD: Yoichi Komatsu
D: Akira Yamada
P: Takashi Homma
CW: Hideo Fujimoto
DF: Ooparts
A: Asatsu Inc.

1: I wear a kimono with the right side under the left, wear the right shoe on the left foot and the left shoe on the right foot, put on a hakama with the front side back, and ride a horse facing its rump. My favorite things are those which are hated by others. In particular, I dislike to be like-minded. Objection is the only credit in life. Raising an objection makes a life worth living. Objection gives a chance to understand myself. I am Mitsuharu Kaneko."Objection!"

きものは左前、靴は右左、袴はうしろ前、馬には尻をむいて乗る。人のいやがるものこそ、僕の好物。とりわけ嫌ひは、気の揃ふといふことだ。僕は信じる。反対こそ、人生で唯一つ立派なことだと。反対こそ生きてることだ。反対こそじぶんをつかむことだ。金子光晴"反対"

2: A newness is always created by those who will not take an opportunist attitude. Spoon hopes to stick to be original. Now, the pad on the reverse side of the Silicon Pad Belt produces the comfortable sense of fitness just like being united with the wrist. The Watch for those who stick to originality.

新しいものはいつも迎合しない人から生まれる。スプーンはオリジナルであることにこだわりたい。今度はシリコンパッドベルトの裏のパッドが手首との一体感と快い装着感を生むのだ。オリジナルであることにこだわる人の時計。

CIA43-2011 ¥35,000 (without tax) with Eco-Drive produced by **CITIZEN**

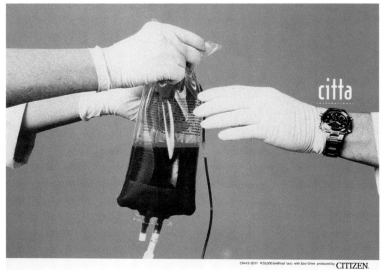

CIA43-2011 ¥35,000 (without tax) with Eco-Drive produced by **CITIZEN**

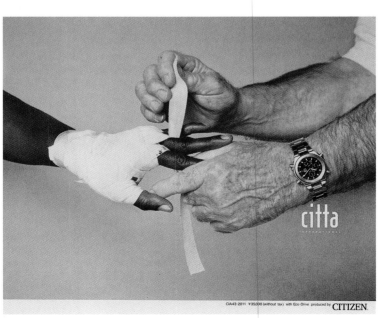

CIA43-2011 ¥35,000 (without tax) with Eco-Drive produced by **CITIZEN**

Citizen Trading Co., Ltd.
Watch Manufacturer
時計製造販売
Japan 1998
CD: Akira Kurosawa
D: Gen Ishii
P: Hibiki Kobayashi
CW: Tomomi Maeda
A: Hakuhodo Inc.

Seiko Corp.
Watch Manufacturer 時計製造販売
Japan 1997
CD: Keiji Tsuji
AD, D: Yoshito Kubota
D: Shigemasa Tatsumi
P: Takashi Sekiguchi
CW: Takeru Makuuchi
DF: Rings
A: Asatsu Inc.

1: Go beyond brains.
脳を超えろ。
2: I'm not you.
私は、君ではない。
3: Want to know what time it is?
いま何時か、知りたい？

Citizen Trading Co., Ltd.
Watch Manufacturer 時計製造販売
Japan 1997
CD, CW: Hitoshi Nagasawa
AD, D: Satoru Shimizu（1,2）/ Katsunori Nishi（3）
P: Toshinobu Kobayashi

Seiko Corp.
Watch Manufacturer 時計製造販売
Japan 1997
CD: Shigeki Yamakado (sgt Inc.)
AD: Masami Shimizu
D: Takashi Kawazoe
PD: Kayoko Komatsu (sgt Inc.)
I: Jeffrey Fulvimari
CW: Ben Uozumi
A: Dentsu Inc.

Egocentric. Deua. / わがままデューア。

Swatch Store
Watch Store
時計販売店
USA 1998
CD, AD: Andrew Janson
D, P: Maciek Pinno
CW: Eric Sorenson
A: Benenson Janson

Seiko Corp.
Watch Manufacturer
時計製造販売
Japan 1997
CD: Satoru Yokokawa
AD, D: Yoichi Komatsu
D: Tamon Saito
P: Naka
CW: Hideo Fujimoto
A: Asatsu Inc.

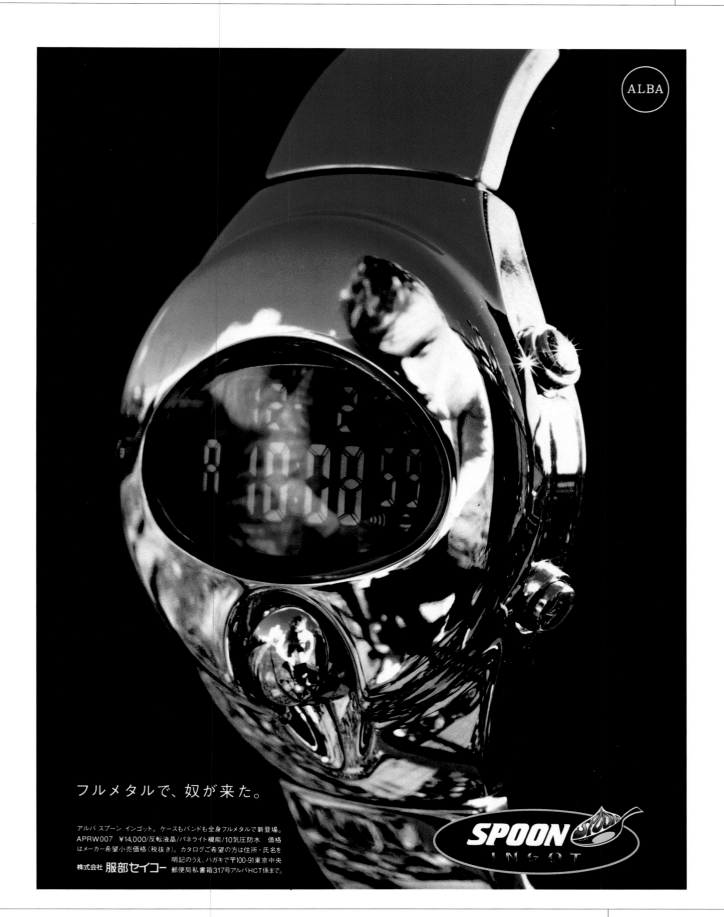

ALBA

フルメタルで、奴が来た。

アルバ スプーン インゴット。ケースもバンドも全身フルメタルで新登場。
APRW007 ¥14,000/反転液晶/バネライト機能/10気圧防水 価格
はメーカー希望小売価格（税抜き）。カタログご希望の方は住所・氏名を
明記のうえ、ハガキで〒100-91東京中央
郵便局私書箱317号アルバHCT係まで。
株式会社 服部セイコー

SPOON
INGOT

He's here, in full metal. / フルメタルで、奴が来た。

Seiko Corp.
Watch Manufacturer
時計製造販売
Japan 1996
CD: Satoru Yokokawa
AD, D: Yoichi Komatsu
D: Tamon Saito
P: Naoki Tsuruta
A: Asatsu Inc.

Nike
Sports Apparel Maker
スポーツ用品メーカー
Brazil 1997
CD: Dan Wieden
AD: Robert Nakata
P: Stock
CW: Glenn Cole

1: Create / Destroy
創造する。/ 破壊する。
2: Remember why you started
貴方がなぜ始めたかということを思い出せ。
3: Lead the faithful
信じる者達のリーダーになれ

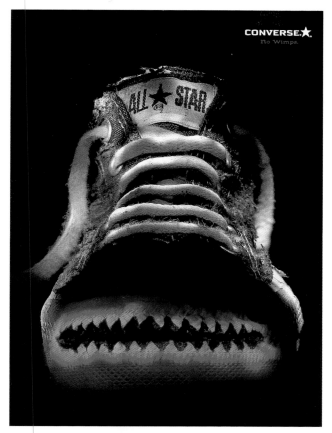

Converse
Sports Shoes Maker
スポーツシューズメーカー
Thailand 1996
CD: Amorn Harinnitisuk
AD: Chatchavong Prayudrat
P: Nimith Siriprechapong
CW: Rachavadee Ngamsanga
A: Ogilvy & Mather

Nike
Sports Apparel Maker
スポーツ用品メーカー
Italy / Netherlands 1997
CD: Jon Matthews / Charlotte Moore
AD: Robert Nakata
P: Hans Pieterse (Product) / Stock
I, D: Souverein (Paintbox)
CW: Glenn Cole
A: Wieden & Kennedy Amsterdam

Nike
Sports Apparel Maker
スポーツ用品メーカー
Netherlands 1997
CD: Jon Matthews
AD: John Norman
D, I, Typographer: Harmine Louwe
P: Yani (3) / Stock
CW: Kathleen Lane
A: Wieden & Kennedy Amsterdam

1,2: do running / 走れ
3: abuse adrenaline / アドレナリンを乱用しろ
4: make your own chemicals / 自分の体でケミカルを作れ

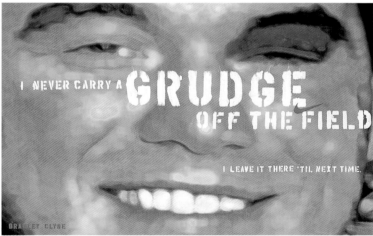

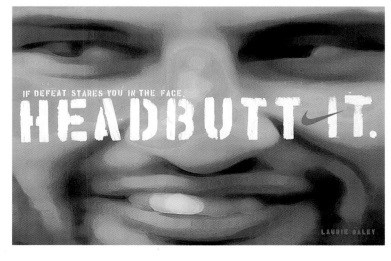

1
2 3
4

1: It's only the most brutal team sport
in the world if they can tackle you.
タックルされる時だけが、世界一野蛮な
チーム・スポーツだ。
2: There's not always next week
必ず来週が来るわけではない
3: I never carry a grudge off the field.
I leave it there 'til next time
フィールドの外に恨みは持ち出さない
次回までそこに置きっぱなしだ
4: If defeat stares you in the face, headbutt it.
敗北に取りつかれたら、頭突きでなぎ倒せ。

Nike
Sports Apparel Maker
スポーツ用品メーカー
Australia 1997
CD: Jim Riswold / John Jay
AD: Linda Knight
I: Patty Fork
CW: Andy McKeon
A: Wieden & Kennedy

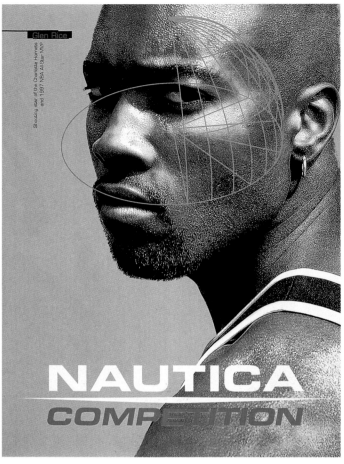

Glen Rice

Shooting star of the Charlotte Hornets
and 1997 NBA All-Star MVP

Nautica Apparel Inc.
Sports Apparel Maker
スポーツ用品メーカー
Japan 1998
CD, AD: David Chu
D: Anne Taylor Davis
P: Claws Wickrath
DF: Anne Taylor Davis Communications

Push the limit / さらに限界まで。

Reebok Japan, Inc.
Sports Apparel Maker
スポーツ用品メーカー
Japan 1997
Associate CD: Isao Mochizuki
AD, D: Koichi Shigaya / Nobuaki Hongo
P: Kazunari Koyama
CG Operator: Tadashi Saito
CW: Yuko Machida
Art: Jun Watanabe
A: Leo Burnett - Kyodo Co., Ltd.

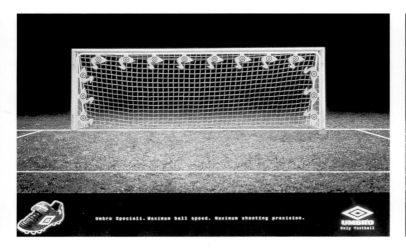

1: **Umbro**
Sports Shoes Maker
スポーツシューズメーカー
Brazil 1998
CD: Alexandre Gama
AD: Rogerio Lima
P: Mario Fontes
CW: Marcelo Sato
A: Young & Rubicam Brasil

2,3,4,5: **Umbro**
Sports Shoes Maker
スポーツシューズメーカー
Brazil 1997-98
CD, AD, CW: Alexandre Gama
P: Hilton Ribeiro (2,3,4,5) / Marcos César (3,4,5)
A: Young & Rubicam Brasil

1 2
3 4
5 6

1: We see a long pass through the field.
私達はフィールドを横切るロングパスをみました。
2: We see a striker totally free of marking.
私達はストライカーが完全にマークを抜けたのをみました。
3: We see a defender marking the striker.
私達はディフェンダーがストライカーをマークしているのをみました。
4: We see an offensive midfield breaking into the defense.
私達は攻撃側ミッドフィールドがディフェンスを突き破るのをみました。
5: We see a fullback who got the red card.
私達はフルバックにレッドカードが出るのをみました。
6: We see a wing coming from behind the fullback.
私達はフルバックの後ろからウィングが出てくるのをみました。

Umbro
Sports Shoes Maker
スポーツシューズメーカー
Brazil 1997
CD, AD, CW: Alexandre Gama
P: Keystone（1）/ Photonica（2,5,6）/
Arnaldo Pappalardo（3,4）
A: Young & Rubicam Brasil

IS YOUR
DAUGHTER HOME?

AFTERNOON
OFFICER.

1 2

Bugaboos Eyewear
Eyewear Manufacturer　メガネ製造販売
Canada　1997
CD, CW: Chris Staples
CD, AD: Mark Mizgala
P: Leon Behar
Digital Artist: Nancy Joyce
A: Palmer Jarvis DDB

1: Is your daughter home? /お嬢さん、います？
2: Afternoon, officer. / こんにちは、おまわりさん

流行を追うランナー、または敗者について。

この冬は、

汗で濡れた

シャツと

紫の唇

が

おしゃれ。

気温が低い冬のランニングであっても汗をかくことは避けられない。冬の汗は冷たい外気にさらされて、貴重な体温を冷酷にも奪い去る厄介ものだ。私たちが独自に開発した機能素材、ナイキ DRI-F.I.T.ならば、汗を素早く吸い取って、外部へ発散。あなたにサラサラ快適な運動環境を提供する。これで涼しい顔をしてまるか、それとも、ブルブル寒い顔をして、おしゃれに命をかけてみるか、コースはひとつだ。

クライミング、そして秋山の魅力について。

山の女神との

ロマンスは

素晴らしい。

身も凍る

ような結末

さえなければ。

秋山は、美しく、ロマンチックで、そして冷酷だ。美顔を装っていた自然は、突然凶暴な牙をむく、標高2000mで冷たい復讐を浴びれば、あなたは氷点下の年獄に幽閉される。無防備な姿でこの状況に遭遇することは何を意味するか。だから、私たちはナイキ サーマ-F.I.T.を開発した。独自のマイクロファイバー素材が、軽量にして最大限の断熱性を発揮、厳しい寒さに対し、クライマーの体温を暖かく保ち、エネルギーのロスを防ぐ。そう、秋山を天国にするのも地獄にするのも女神ではない、あなた自身なのだ。

1: This winter, fashionable are shirts wet with sweat and purple lips.
この冬は、汗で濡れたシャツと紫の唇がおしゃれ。
2: Romance with a mountain goddess is wonderful unless it leads to a chilly ending.
山の女神とのロマンスは素晴らしい。身も凍るような結末さえなければ。

Nike Japan
Sports Apparel Maker
スポーツ用品メーカー
Japan 1997
CD: Larry Fray
AD: Seiji Shiramizu（1）/ Yukio Okada（2）
P: Fujio Saimon
CW: Hisamu Yamada
A: McCann-Erickson Inc. / Wieden & Kennedy

友達はオオイ。愛と平和が大切。彼女とは、けんかはしない。ブランドより自分が好きかきらいかで選ぶ。お金はやっぱりとてもほしい。ベルトモはいない。コンビニに行くと涙が少しでる。俺はここにいるよ。

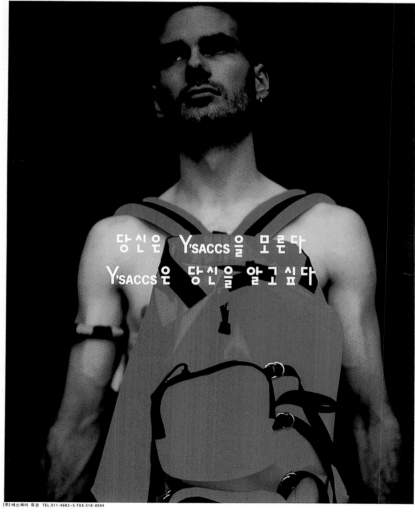

1: Nike
Sports Apparel Maker
スポーツ用品メーカー
USA / Japan 1997
CD: Jim Riswold / John Jay
AD: Linda Knight
P: Kurt Markus
CW: Mike McCommon
A: Wieden & Kennedy

2: Y'saccs Corp.
Bag Manufacturer
バッグメーカー
Japan 1997
AD: Tomohiko Nagakura
D: Yasuko Uchie
P: Naoki Tsuruta
Stylist: Koichiro Yamamoto
CW: Yasuhiko Sakura
A: Sun-Ad Co., Ltd.

2: I have a lot of friends. Precious things are love and peace. I don't quarrel with my girlfriend. I make a choice not by brand but by my own taste. I awfully want money as well. I have no friend to communicate through a pager. When I go to a convenient store, tears come to my eyes a little. Here I am.
友達はオオイ。愛と平和が大切。彼女とは、けんかはしない。ブランドより自分が好きかきらいかで選ぶ。お金はやっぱりとてもほしい。ベルトモはいない。コンビニに行くと涙が少しでる。俺はここにいるよ。

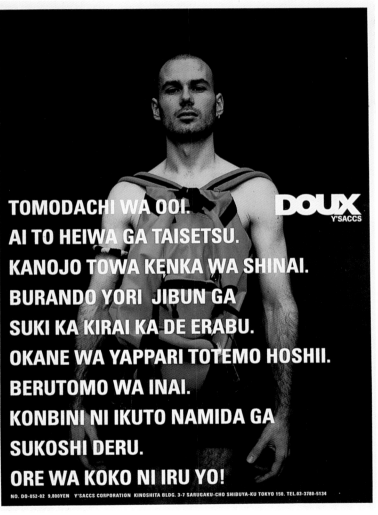

Daniel Franck * Mantis

MANTIS

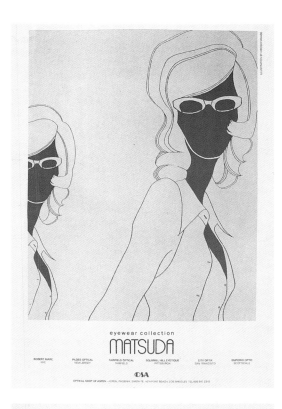

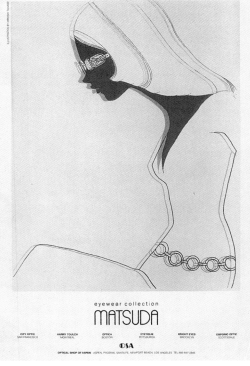

1 2

1: **Optical Shop of Aspen**
Eyewear Sales
眼鏡卸販売店
USA / Japan 1997
AD: Hideki Nakajima
D: Yukio Kobayashi
I: Hiroshi Tanabe

2: **Paul Smith Ltd.**
Apparel Maker
アパレルメーカー
Japan / UK 1997
AD: Alan Aboud (Aboud·Sodano)
P: Sandro Sodano (Aboud·Sodano)

Shellys Shoes
Shoe Retailer
靴販売店
UK 1996
CD: John Merriman
AD: Rob Neilson
P: Dave Stewart
CW: Ben Jones
A: Mustoe Merrimaw Herring Levy

1: Did he jump or was he pushed? Either way he had nothing worth living for, and they knew it.
あいつは飛び込んだのか、それとも押されたのか。どっちにしても、生きるあてがなかったんだ。みんな知ってる。
2: He had never really fitted in, and deep down they all knew they were responsible.
あいつは1度もサイズが合ったことがなかった。みんな自分の責任だってことがよくわかってた。
3: When they realised they weren't created in his image, they lost all hope.
あいつのイメージで作り出されたんじゃないことがわかって、希望をなくしたんだ。

1 2
3 4

1: Everyone RSVP'd. The forecast was clear skies. And the kids kept their fingers out of the cake. See, LOVE DOES CONQUER ALL.
招待状の返事が届き、天気予報は晴れ。ウェディング・ケーキを前にじっとがまんしている子供たち。……そう、愛があれば、どんな問題も乗り越えられるのです。

2: The candles were luminous. The ring sparkled. And your mom even stopped crying. See, LOVE DOES CONQUER ALL.
揺らめくキャンドルの炎。キラリと光る薬指のリング。そっと目頭を押さえる花嫁の母。……そう、愛があれば、どんな問題も乗り越えられるのです。

3: The florist showed up early . The choir rang out like angels. And you hardly flinched saying "I do". See, LOVE DOES CONQUER ALL.
式場を埋め尽くす花々。聖歌隊の天使のような歌声。自信に満ちた誓いの言葉。……そう、愛があれば、どんな問題も乗り越えられるのです。

4: The guests danced. The champagne flowed. And your father actually forgot how much money he spent. See, LOVE DOES CONQUER ALL.
ダンスを楽しむ招待客。なみなみと注がれるシャンパン。費用のことなどすっかり忘れている花嫁の父。……そう、愛があれば、どんな問題も乗り越えられるのです。

Beverly Clark Collection
Bridal Products Company
ブライダル用品メーカー
USA 1998
CD, AD, D: Andrew Janson
D: Maciek Pinno
P: Ron Derhacopian / Christianna Ceppes
CW: Eric Sorenson
A: Benenson Janson

Wallis Womenswear
Womenswear Retailer
婦人服販売
UK 1997
CD: Graham Watson / Bruce Crouch
AD: Steve Hudson
CW: Victoria Fallon
P: Bob Carlos Clarke
Typographer: Andy Bird
A: Bartle Bogle Hegarty Ltd.

Guess? Inc.
Apparel Maker
アパレルメーカー
USA 1997
AD: Paul Marciano
D: Kumiko Morishita
P: Dah Len
DF: Guess? Advertising

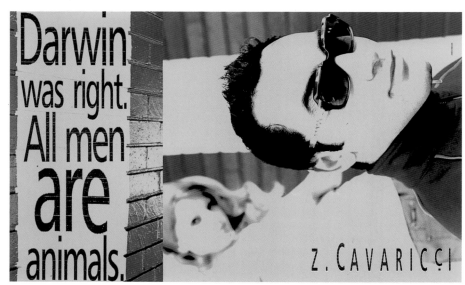

Z. Cavaricci
Apparel Maker　アパレルメーカー
USA　1996
CD, AD, D: Andrew Janson
AD: Howard Benenson
P: James Smolka
CW: Eric Sorenson / Mick Di Maria
A: Benenson Janson

1: No one's gonna spot you across a crowded room and say, "Wow! Nice personality!"
人混みのなかで「あいつ、性格いいじゃん」なんて出会いはあり得ない。
2: He just wanted a little spark to their life. She decided on a blow torch.
彼はちょっとした刺激が欲しかった。彼女は燃え尽きてもいいと思った。
3: It's ok to check out the menu. Just make sure you eat at home.
メニューは見せてあげる。でも、食べるのは家に帰ってからにして。
4: Darwin was right. All men are animals.
ダーウィンは正しかった。男はみんな獣だ。

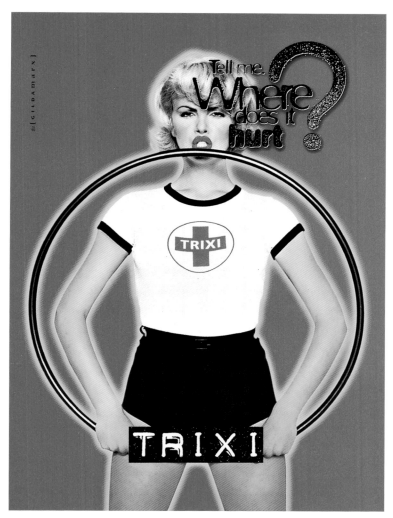

1: Tell me where does it hurt?
どこが痛いの？教えて。
2: Obviously she aroused more than his curiosity.
彼女が彼に好奇心以上の気持ちを芽生えさせたことは明らかだ。
3: He used to brag about his self control.
彼は自分の自制心を誇りに思っていた。

Trixi
Apparel Maker
アパレルメーカー
USA 1996
CD, AD, D: Andrew Janson
D: Howard Benenson
P: Moshe Brakha
CW: Barbie Gordon
A: Benenson Janson

it's my party

at chelsea hotel in the tuesday afternoon. Adriana, Myka and Freddy meet the party. photographed by Ellen von Unwerth for trans continents.

Trans Continents（Millennium Japan）
Apparel Maker
アパレルメーカー
Japan 1998
CD, AD: Trans Continents (Millennium Japan)
P: Ellen Von Unwerth

Trans Continents (Millennium Japan)
Apparel Maker
アパレルメーカー
Japan 1997
CD, AD: Trans Continents (Millennium Japan)
P: David Lachapelle

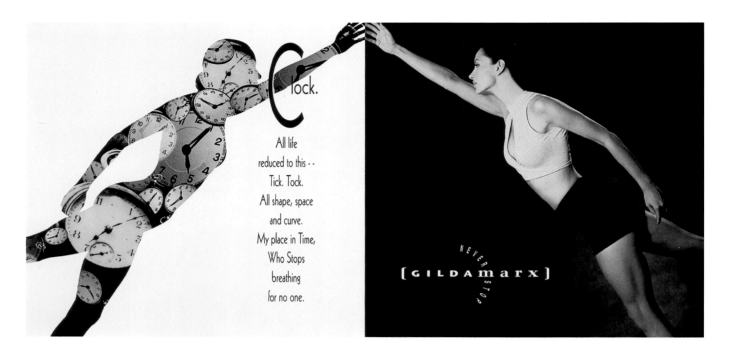

Gilda Marx
Apparel Maker
アパレルメーカー
USA 1996
CD, AD, D: Andrew Janson
D: Howard Benenson
P: Suzanne Nyerges
CW: Mick Di Maria
A: Benenson Janson

1: Clock. All life reduced to this ... Tick.Tock. All shape, space and curve. My place in Time, Who Stops breathing for no one.
時計。この世のあらゆる営みは、カチッカチッカチッと刻まれる一瞬に集約される。どんな形も、どんな空間もどんな曲線も。その一瞬が私の居場所。誰のためでもなく自分自身のために生きる私の。
2: After Searching, it is now,when I'm not looking, do I find myself and like what I see.
探し続けたからこそ今の私がある。目を閉じていては、自分を見つけることも何かを好きになることもない。
3: Wind. Ever changing. Never ending. Always finding someplace new. An eternal journey to discover my true self.
風。とどまることなく絶えることなくいつも新しい場所を求めて。本当の私を見つけるための終わりのない旅。

きょ年の服では、恋もできない。

踊れるバーバリー。

Burberrys
OF LONDON
BLUE LABEL

Photographer : Patrick Demarchelier

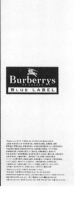

バリバリのバーバリー。

Burberrys
BLUE LABEL

失恋は、何度やってもやめられない。

Burberrys
BLUE LABEL

1: I just can't be in love wearing last year's clothes.
きょ年の服では、恋もできない。
2: Burn-it-up Burberrys
バリバリのバーバリー。
3: My heart's been broken so many times but I just can't stop.
失恋は、何度やってもやめられない。

Sanyo Shokai Ltd.
Apparel Maker
アパレルメーカー
Japan 1996-97
CD, CW: Jun Maki
CD, AD: Masatoshi Toda
D: Koichi Kuno
P: Patrick Demarchelier(1)/ Matthew Rolston(2,3)

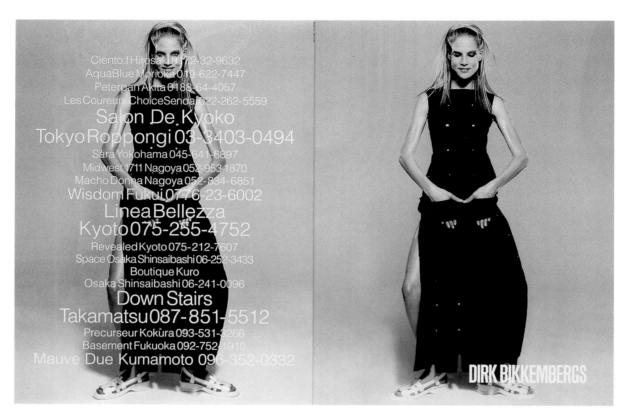

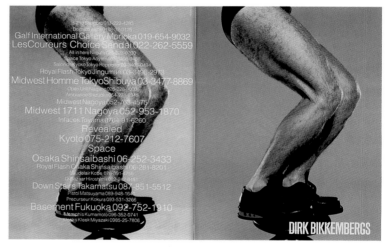

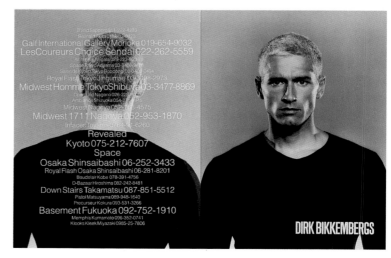

Dirk Bikkembergs
Apparel Maker
アパレルメーカー
Japan 1998
CD: Dirk Bikkembergs
P: Michel Comte

**MARITHÉ
+
FRANÇOIS
GIRBAUD**

(株)TAKAYA SHOJI INC. GIRBAUD DIVISION 03-5489-4381
TOKYO:03-3477-1313/OSAKA:06-644-2523/KOBE:078-360-2993/NAGOYA:052-261-9527

**MARITHÉ
FRANÇOIS
GIRBAUD**

jeans

INFORMATION&カタログ請求：TAKAYA SHOJI INC.03-3961-9181
BE11 SHOP：TOKYO.03-3401-6177 IE PLAZA246.3-11 MINAMI-AOYAMA,MINATO-KU
SHOP：OSAKA.06-644-2523/NAGOYA.052-261-9527/KOBE.078-360-2993/KYOTO.075-253-3125

Takaya S
Apparel Ma
アパレルメー
Japan 199

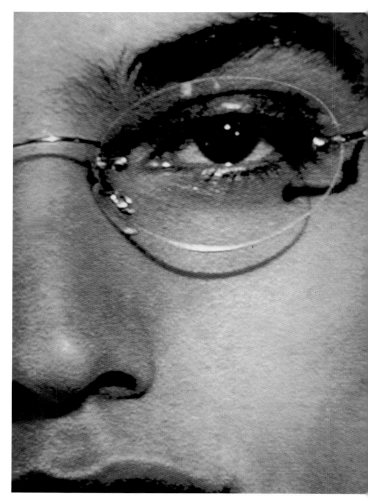

Gucci
Apparel Maker
アパレルメーカー
Italy 1997
AD, D: Lee Swillingham
D: Stuart Spalding
P: Mario Testino

TOKYO

SENDAI

NAGOYA

TOYAMA

OSAKA

ORIZZONTI CO.,LTD.
Tel.03-3404-7185

Vivienne Westwood
Apparel Maker
アパレルメーカー
UK / Japan 1998
CD, AD, D: Vivienne Westwood
P: Gianpaolo Barbieri

...he was crude, hard, un-educated. He didn't belong in Lady De Beauvoir's world. But she liked him, and buying him nice clothes was a step in the right direction.

Poor Greg from accounts failed to realise that attractive Lucinda was only interested in the handsome stranger cutting a dash in the Paul Smith outfit.

1,2: **Paul Smith Ltd.**
Apparel Maker
アパレルメーカー
Japan / UK 1995
AD: Alan Aboud (Aboud・Sodano)
I: L. Houghton

3: **Paul Smith Ltd.**
Apparel Maker
アパレルメーカー
Japan / UK 1996
AD: Alan Aboud (Aboud・Sodano)
I: Maxine Law @ A/S

1: ...he was crude, hard, un-educated. He didn't belong in Lady De Beauvoir's world. But she liked him, and buying him nice clothes was a step in the right direction.
粗野で図々しく教養もない、フェミニストとはほど遠い男。でも、悪くないわ。彼女は思った。いい服を着せたら、かなりいける。

2: Poor Greg from accounts failed to realise that attractive Lucinda was only interested in the handsome stranger cutting a dash in the Paul Smith outfit.
勘定を払い終えたグレッグは、愛しいルシンダの視線がポール・スミスで決めた見知らぬ男に釘づけだとは、まったく気づいていなかった。

You walk past and the poor guy can't sleep for days.

HYP∃

A div. of Harkham Ind.

2: You walk past and the poor guy can't sleep for days.
前を通りすぎたら、彼は2、3日眠れない。

1: **Issey Miyake Inc.**
Apparel Maker
アパレルメーカー
Japan 1998
CD: Anne de Maupou
AD: Pierre-Yves Demarck
P: Philippe Pollet-Villars
CW: Valérie Larrondo
DF: CLM / BBDO

2: **Hype**
Apparel Maker
アパレルメーカー
USA 1994
CD: Andrew Janson
AD: Chad Squirmer
CW: David Bradley
A: Andrew Janson & Associates

Laforet Harajuku Co., Ltd.
Fashion Retail Building
ファッションビル
Japan 1997
CD, AD, D: Takuya Onuki
DF: Onuki Design

Nude or Laforet. / ヌードかラフォーレ

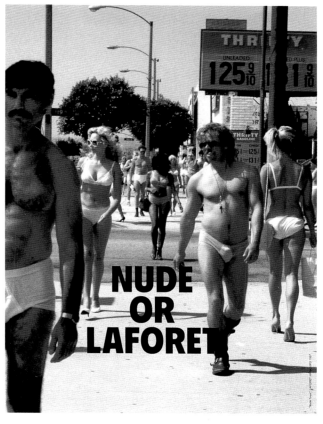

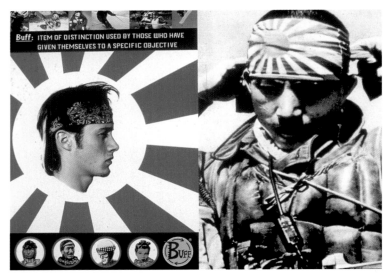

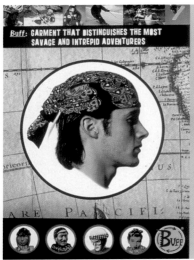

Caviro S. L.
Apparel Maker
アパレルメーカー
Spain 1998
CD: Quim Calvo
CD, AD: Karlos Vives
I: Xavier Font
CW: Victor Muntanya
A: Frank & Enstein

1: Item of distinction used by those who have given themselves to a specific objective.
特殊任務に就く決意の証として。
2: Garment that distinguishes the most savage and intrepid adventurers.
タフで恐れを知らぬ冒険者の証として。
3: Protective element used by warriors on the battlefield.
戦場で自分の身を守るために。
4: Decorative ornament used by some tribes to differentiate themselves from the others.
他の部族と区別を付けるために。

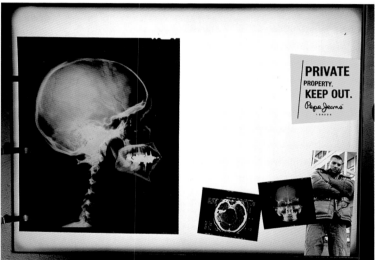

1: Things to do today.
きょうしなければならないこと
2: Private property. Keep out.
私有地につき立入禁止
3: Outside every thin girl there's a fat guy trying to get in.
スマートなギャルの回りで必ずデブの男が入ろうとしてる
4: People who exercise just die healthier.
運動する人はもっと健康になって死ぬだけ
5: Practice safe sex. Get a virgin.
安全なセックスを実践しよう。バージンをゲット。

Pepe Jeans
Apparel Maker
アパレルメーカー
UK 1996
CD: Tim Delaney
AD: Dave Beverley
P: Laurie Haskell
CW: Rob Burleigh
DF: Leagas Delaney

Evis Industry Ltd.
Apparel Maker
アパレルメーカー
Japan / UK 1997

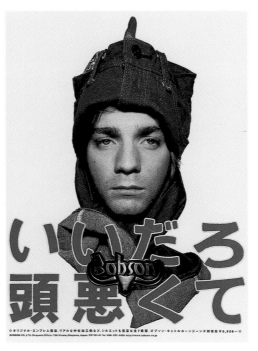

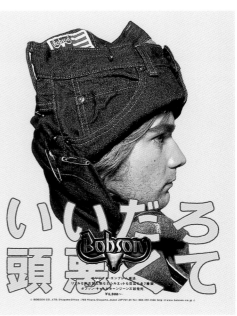

I'm stupid, so what? / いいだろ頭悪くて

Bobson Co., Ltd.
Apparel Maker　アパレルメーカー
Japan 1997
CD: Kiyoshi Kudo
AD: Yoshimasa Hiramatsu
D: Hiroshi Matsumura / Kayoko Maeda
P: Masao Chiba
CW: Kotaro Yoshioka
DF: Birth Company
A: Hakuhodo Inc., Kansai Branch

Diesel
Apparel Maker
アパレルメーカー
UK 1998
CD: Paul Weinberger
AD: Steve Williams
P: Erwin Olaf / Zac Macaulay (Underwater Shot)
CW: Adrian Lim
A: Lowe Howard-Spink

1: Boot cut, loose , skin tight, or flared, our jeans come in over 10 different fits and up to 5 leg lengths. Because you never know when a 7 foot woman with bow legs and a pot belly is going to walk into your store.
ブーツカットもルーズも、スキンタイトもフレアも、Dieselのジーンズのフィットは10種類以上。丈も5種類。いつなんどき、O脚で太鼓腹で身長7フィートの女性が来るかもしれませんから。

2: Loose fitting pants, cut low on the waist, triple stitched for extra strength. Our workwear suits labourers, clubbers, murderers, or anyone else who needs lots of odd shaped pockets.
ルーズフィット・パンツ。ウエストは浅めにカット。丈夫な三重ステッチ。Dieselの作業服は、労働者の皆さん、クラバーと殺人者の方々、その他どなたでも、変な形のポケットがいっぱい欲しい人にぴったり。

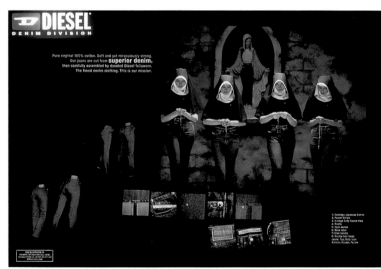

3: Dump the chocolate fudge ice-cream, hide the burgers, shed that excess weight. It'll all be worth it for our slim fit jackets. They're tailored tight on the body, and longer in the sleeves. Remember, no pain, no gain.
チョコレートアイスなんか捨てて、ハンバーガーなんか隠して、余分な体重を落としましょう。スリムフィット・ジャケットを着るためなら。貴方のボディにぴったりフィット、そで丈も長め。努力なければ成果なし。

4: Over 10 styles of legwear, 8 weights of cloth, 24 different washes. Everything from streaky to sandblasted. They're not your first jeans but they could be your last. At least you'll leave a beautiful corpse.
スタイルは10以上、生地の重さ8種、ウォッシュは24種類。ストリークからサンドブラストまで何でも揃うDieselのジーンズ。Dieselは、あなたの初めてのジーンズではないかもしれません。でも、きっと最後のジーンズになるでしょう。少なくともカッコいい死体は残せるというわけです。

5: Only the finest quality 12 1/2oz denim is good enough for Diesel. This is overdyed, then washed, and finally distressed. The result is antique dirty denim which has an aged, vintage appearance. A bit like your grandmother.
Dieselが選ぶのは最高級の121/2oz デニムだけ。染めて、洗って、最後にくたびれさせて。それはもうアンティークな汚れデニム。どこかおばあちゃんを思わせる、年代もの、ビンテージの風合いです。

6: Pure virginal 100% cotton. Soft and yet miraculously strong. Our jeans are cut from superior denim, then carefully assembled by devoted Diesel followers. The finest denim clothing. This is our mission.
混じりけなしの綿100%。ソフトなのに驚くほど丈夫。最高級のデニムをカットして、Dieselの献身的な職人が縫製したジーンズ。最高のデニム衣料。それが我々の使命。

Diesel
Apparel Maker
アパレルメーカー
UK 1998
CD: Paul Weinberger
AD: Gary Anderson
P: Sandro Sodano
CW: Tony Miller
A: Lowe Howard-Spink

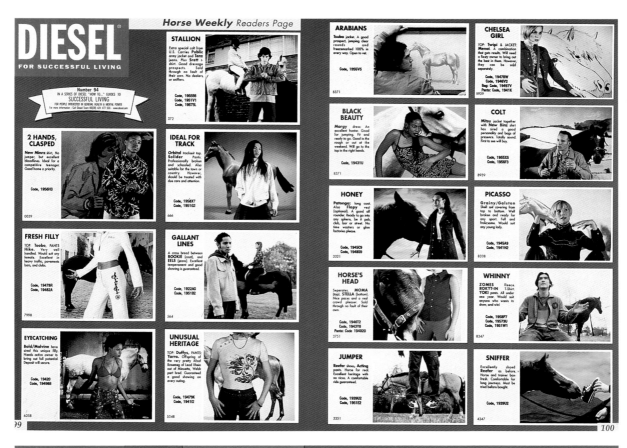

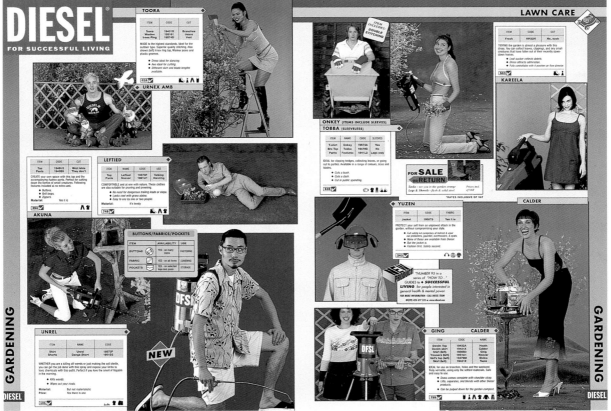

HD Lee
Apparel Maker　アパレルメーカー
South Africa　1997
CD, CW: Christo Nel
AD: Benoit Ruscoe
P: Barry Downard
I: Jason Juta
DF: Matthews & Charter, O & M

1: It must have an ageless quality.
　永遠のクオリティをもつこと
2: The idea must be simple to pull off.
　成功を収めるにはシンプルなアイディアであること

3: It must reflect the shape of things to come.
次の世代の形を表現すること。
4: Always allow room for improvement
常に改善の余地を残すこと
5: The customer is King.
お客様は神様

Levi Strauss
Apparel Maker
アパレルメーカー
UK 1997
CD: John Hegarty
AD: Rosie Arnold
CW: Will Awdry
P: Nadav Kander
Typographer: Andy Bird
A: Bartle Bogle Hegarty Ltd.

Levi Strauss
Apparel Maker
アパレルメーカー
UK 1997
CD: John Hegarty
AD: Adam Chiappe
CW: Matthew Saunby
P: Kevin Summers
Typographer: Jeff Merrels
Sculptors: Steve Furlonger / Terry New
(Windsor Workshop)
A: Bartle Bogle Hegarty Ltd.

Levi Strauss Japan
Apparel Maker
アパレルメーカー
UK / Japan 1997
CD: Stanley Wong (BBH Asia-Pacific)
AD: Jason Stewart
CW: Brian Cooper
P: Platon
A: Bartle Bogle Hegarty Ltd.

No two pairs are the same. / 同じようで、同じではない。

Levi's jeans modelled
by original wearers.
Models : Sonny, 60, Sterling, 62,
and Rusty 71, Ranchers.
Items : 505 stiohy jeans.
Stylist : Simon Foxton.
Photographer : Nick Knight.

Levi's jeans modelled
by original wearer.
Model : Lloyd, 79, rancher, Colorado.
Item : 561 cinchback jeans.
Stylist : Simon Foxton.
Photographer : Nick Knight.

Levi's jacket modelled
by original wearer.
Model : Alonzo, 66, cowboy, Colorado.
Item : Type-II jacket.
Stylist : Simon Foxton.
Photographer : Nick Knight.

Levi Strauss Europe
Apparel Maker
アパレルメーカー
UK 1996
CD: John Hegarty
AD: Steve Hudson
P: Nick Knight
CW: Victoria Fallon
A: Bartle Bogle Hegarty Ltd.

Levi's shirt modelled
by original wearer.
Model : Julius, 89, rancher, Colorado.
Items : Sawtooth shirt and 517 relaxed fit jeans.
Stylist : Simon Foxton.
Photographer : Nick Knight.

Levi's jeans modelled
by original wearer.
Model : Josephine, 78, teacher, Colorado.
Item : 534 women's fit jeans.
Stylist : Simon Foxton.
Hair : Kevin Ryan.
Photographer : Nick Knight.

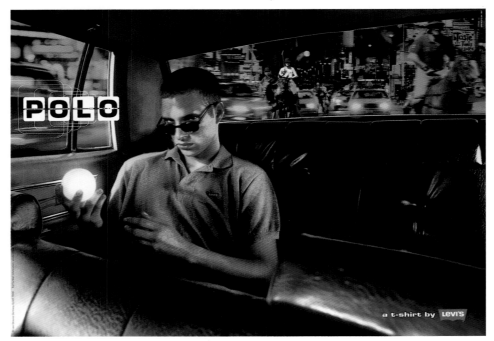

Levi Strauss Germany GmbH
Apparel Maker
アパレルメーカー
Germany 1997
CD: Arndt Dallmann (Art) / Guido Heffels (Text)
AD, D, DF: Rainer Kollender (Art)
AD, CW: Thomas Grabinger (Text)
P: Davies & Davies (1,3,7,8,10) / Carli Hermes (2,4) / Garry Owens (5,6,9)
CW, DF: Springer & Jacoby Advertising GmbH

1 2
3
4 5

UNITED COLORS
OF BENETTON.

1

United Colors of Benetton
Apparel Maker
アパレルメーカー
Italy / Japan 1997(1), 98(2)
CD, AD, P: Oliviero Toscani

ALL HUMAN BEINGS
ARE BORN FREE AND EQUAL
IN DIGNITY AND RIGHTS
(art.1)

第一条（自由平等）
すべての人間は、生まれながらにして
自由であり、かつ、
尊厳と権利とについて平等である。

 世界人権宣言50周年
FIFTIETH ANNIVERSARY
OF THE UNIVERSAL
DECLARATION
OF HUMAN RIGHTS

UNITED COLORS
OF BENETTON.

2

start a lip revolution

lip rouge

introducing stila lip rouge. freedom to recreate your lips in one revolutionary pen.
double up with lip color and liner in one sleek liquid stain.

stila
cosmetics

catch the
perfect pout
with stila
lipshine

for moisture and shine, apply stila lip gloss alone or over lipstick with a brush 0.26 oz. 7.5g

stila
cosmetics

perfect
skin
in
a
tube

stilastilastilastil
stila
complete
coverage
makeup
1.4oz 38gm
stilastilastilastil

for a fresh look in foundation slip into complete coverage

stila
cosmetics

put a new
spin
on spring

salsa

tango

stila eye rouge. two in one color. tango pink or salsa peach. for eyes and cheeks.
a modern way to wear brights.

stila
cosmetics

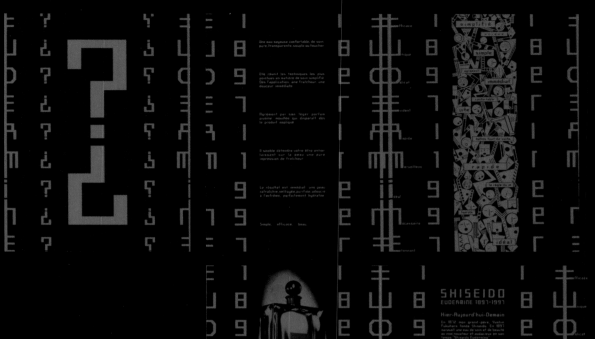

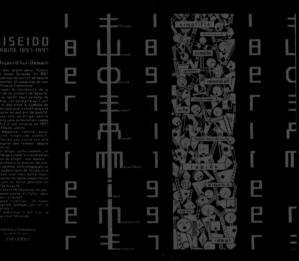

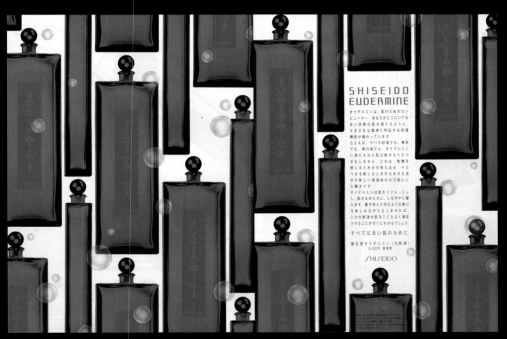

Shiseido Co., Ltd.
Cosmetics Company
化粧品メーカー
Japan 1997
CD: Ikuo Amano
CD, AD: Toshio Yamagata
AD, CW: Serge Lutens
D: Takayasu Yamada / Rie Sakai
P: Seiichi Nakamura
CW: Shoko Yoshida
DF: Shiseido Advertising Creation Department

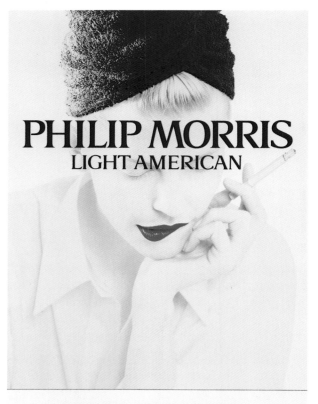

Die EG-Gesundheitsminister: Rauchen gefährdet die Gesundheit. Der Rauch einer Zigarette dieser Marke enthält 0,4 mg Nikotin und 4 mg Kondensat (Teer). (Durchschnittswerte nach ISO)

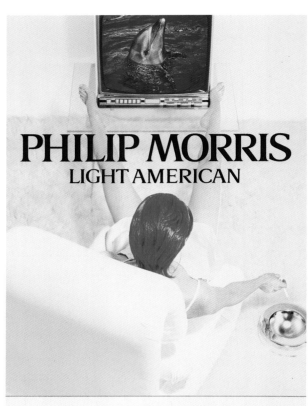

Die EG-Gesundheitsminister: Rauchen gefährdet die Gesundheit. Der Rauch einer Zigarette dieser Marke enthält 0,3 mg Nikotin und 4 mg Kondensat (Teer). (Durchschnittswerte nach ISO)

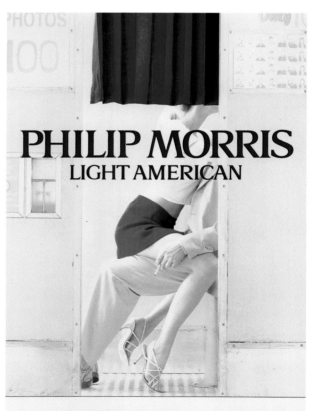

Die EG-Gesundheitsminister: Rauchen gefährdet die Gesundheit. Der Rauch einer Zigarette dieser Marke enthält 0,4 mg Nikotin und 4 mg Kondensat (Teer). (Durchschnittswerte nach ISO)

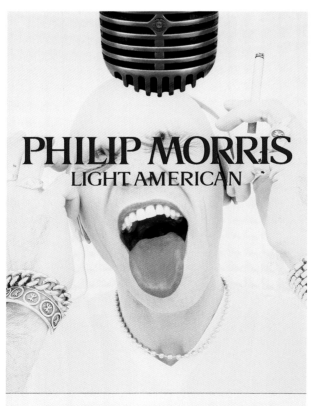

Die EG-Gesundheitsminister: Rauchen gefährdet die Gesundheit. Der Rauch einer Zigarette dieser Marke enthält 0,4 mg Nikotin und 4 mg Kondensat (Teer). (Durchschnittswerte nach ISO)

Philip Morris
Cigarette Manufacturer
たばこ製造販売
Germany 1997
CD, AD: Martina Traut / Roland Gehrmann
P: Stefan Indlekofer (1) / Ralf Mecke (2) / Christian Stoll (3) / Hans Kroeskamp (4,5,8) / Erwin Olaf (6) / Hans Gissinger (7)
A: TBWA Werbeagentur GmbH

1 2 3 4
5 6 7 8

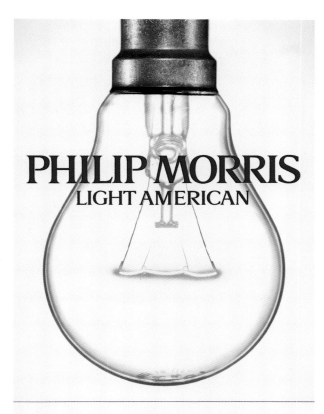

Die EG-Gesundheitsminister: Rauchen gefährdet die Gesundheit. Der Rauch einer Zigarette dieser Marke enthält 0,3 mg Nikotin und 4 mg Kondensat (Teer). (Durchschnittswerte nach ISO)

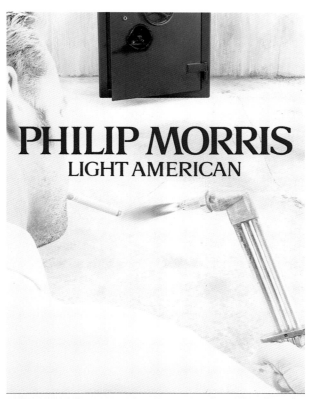

Die EG-Gesundheitsminister: Rauchen gefährdet die Gesundheit. Der Rauch einer Zigarette dieser Marke enthält 0,4 mg Nikotin und 4 mg Kondensat (Teer). (Durchschnittswerte nach ISO)

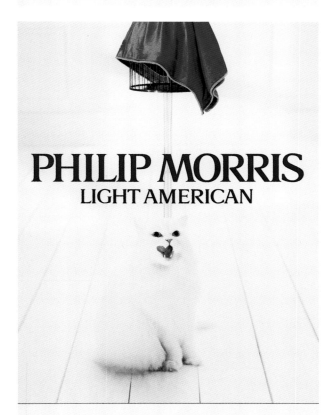

Die EG-Gesundheitsminister: Rauchen gefährdet die Gesundheit. Der Rauch einer Zigarette dieser Marke enthält 0,3 mg Nikotin und 4 mg Kondensat (Teer). (Durchschnittswerte nach ISO)

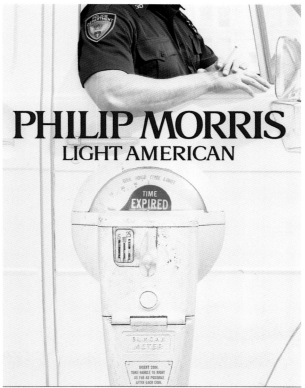

Die EG-Gesundheitsminister: Rauchen gefährdet die Gesundheit. Der Rauch einer Zigarette dieser Marke enthält 0,4 mg Nikotin und 4 mg Kondensat (Teer). (Durchschnittswerte nach ISO)

Advarsel: Sundhedsstyrelsen påpeger, at tobaksrygning er sundhedsskadelig.
Kondensat (tjære) ca. 14 mg. Nikotin ca. 1,2 mg.

Advarsel: Sundhedsstyrelsen påpeger, at tobaksrygning er sundhedsskadelig.
Kondensat (tjære) ca. 14 mg. Nikotin ca. 1,2 mg.

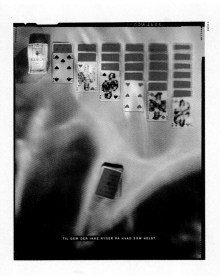

Advarsel: Sundhedsstyrelsen påpeger, at tobaksrygning er sundhedsskadelig.
Kondensat (tjære) ca. 14 mg. Nikotin ca. 1,2 mg.

Advarsel: Sundhedsstyrelsen påpeger, at tobaksrygning er sundhedsskadelig.
Kondensat (tjære) ca. 13 mg. Nikotin ca. 1,2 mg.

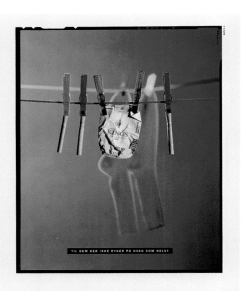

Advarsel: Sundhedsstyrelsen påpeger, at tobaksrygning er sundhedsskadelig.
Kondensat (tjære) ca. 14 mg. Nikotin ca. 1,2 mg.

Advarsel: Sundhedsstyrelsen påpeger, at tobaksrygning er sundhedsskadelig.
Kondensat (tjære) ca. 14 mg. Nikotin ca. 1,2 mg.

House of Prince
Cigarette Manufacturer
たばこ製造販売
Denmark 1996
CD: Fb Borup
AD: Henrik Tvilling
P: Station 1
A: Bates Copenhagen

For those who care about tobacco for what it is.
タバコなら何でもよいとは考えない人のために

Advarsel: Sundhedsstyrelsen påpeger, at tobaksrygning er sundhedsskadelig.
Kondensat (tjære) ca. 14 mg. Nikotin ca. 1,2 mg.

Advarsel: Sundhedsstyrelsen påpeger, at tobaksrygning er sundhedsskadelig.
Kondensat (tjære) ca. 14 mg. Nikotin ca. 1,2 mg.

Advarsel: Sundhedsstyrelsen påpeger, at tobaksrygning er sundhedsskadelig.
Kondensat (tjære) ca. 14 mg. Nikotin ca. 1,2 mg.

Advarsel: Sundhedsstyrelsen påpeger, at tobaksrygning er sundhedsskadelig.
Kondensat (tjære) ca. 14 mg. Nikotin ca. 1,2 mg.

Advarsel: Sundhedsstyrelsen påpeger, at tobaksrygning er sundhedsskadelig.
Kondensat (tjære) ca. 13 mg. Nikotin ca. 1,2 mg.

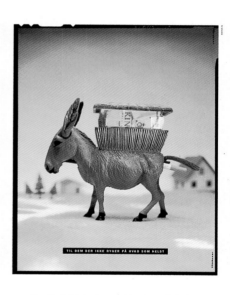

Advarsel: Sundhedsstyrelsen påpeger, at tobaksrygning er sundhedsskadelig.
Kondensat (tjære) ca. 14 mg. Nikotin ca. 1,2 mg.

Vitra GmbH
Furniture Manufacturer
家具製造販売
Germany 1997-98
CD: Moi Soltek
AD: Lutz Pluemecke
P: Matthias Koslik / Uwe Duettmann
CW: Robert Krause
DF: Scholz & Friends Berlin

1: Is it possible for your worktable to move after you ?
　あなたの仕事机はあなたについて移動することができるでしょうか?
2: Anyway, how much of is the work pleasant ?
　そもそも仕事はどれほど楽しいものでしょうか?
3: For those who can not sit in a dream car all day long : New Meda Chair
　一日中夢みたいな車に座っていることができない全ての人々のために：新しいメダ・チェア
4: Please find an utterly new place for the sake of comfort : Your office.
　快適さのために全く新しい場所をみつけてください：あなたのオフィス

Für alle, die nicht den ganzen Tag in ihrem Traumwagen sitzen können: der neue Meda Chair.

Vitra, D-79576 Weil am Rhein, Tel. 0 76 21/7 02-32 08, Fax -34 30. CH-Birsfelden, Tel. 061/377 15 18. A-Wien, Tel. 01/4 05 75 14. http://www.vitra.com, info@vitra.com

Meda Chair, Design: Alberto Meda

vitra.
0 76 21/7 02–32 08

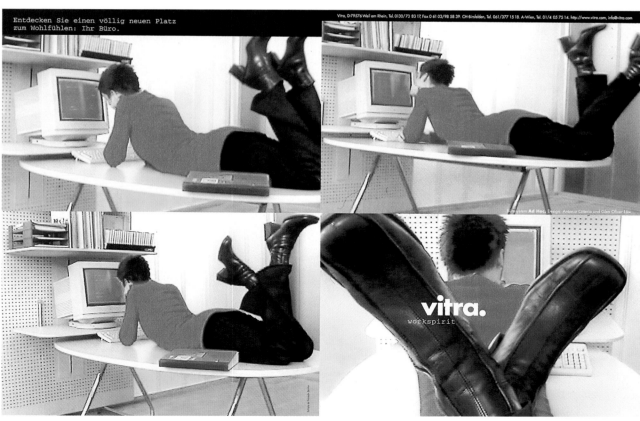

Entdecken Sie einen völlig neuen Platz zum Wohlfühlen: Ihr Büro.

Vitra, D-79576 Weil am Rhein, Tel. 0130/73 83 17, Fax 0 61 03/98 58 39. CH-Birsfelden, Tel. 061/377 15 18. A-Wien, Tel. 01/4 05 75 14. http://www.vitra.com, info@vitra.com

Bürosystem Ad Hoc, Design: Antonio Citterio and Glen Oliver Löw

vitra.
workspirit

3
4

1
2 3

The Body Shop
Cosmetics Company
ボディケア用品・化粧品メーカー
UK 1997
CD, AD, CW: Graeme Norways
AD, CW: Jeff Ford / Gary Sollof
P: Nadav Kander
A: Banc

1: A massage a day keeps the shrink away
　一日一回のマッサージでしなやかな体に。
2: Stress makes you more susceptible to illness
　ストレスは病気への抵抗力を弱めます。
3: De-stress centre
　ストレス解消の場。

Apollo. The new fragrance from Lynx.

OPEN

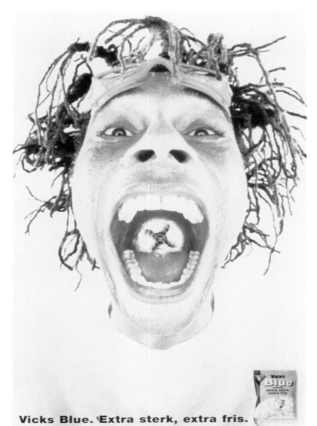

Vicks Blue. Extra sterk, extra fris.

Vicks Blue. Extra sterk, extra fris.

1: **Elida Fabergé**
Cosmetics Company
ヘア・ボディケア用品メーカー
UK 1998
CD: Dennis Lewis
AD: Martin Galton
P: David Hughes
Typographer: Andrew Bird
A: Bartle Bogle Hegarty Ltd.

2: **Procter & Gamble**
Pharmaceutical Company
製薬会社
Netherlands 1997
CD, AD: Raymond Waltjen
AD: Maarten Bakker
P: Jaap Vliegenthart
CW: Herbert van Hoogdalem
A: Noordervliet & Winninghoff / Leo Burnett

1
2

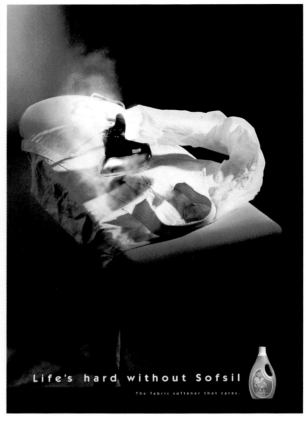

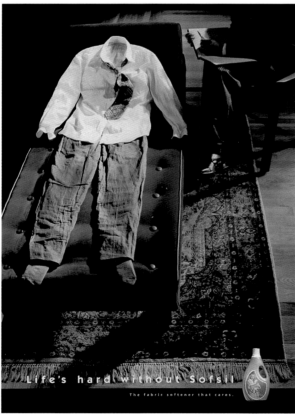

UIC
Household Products Maker
生活用品メーカー
Singapore 1997
CD: Mike Boekholt
AD: Eric Siow
P: Jorg Sunderman
CW: Anna Toosey
A: Bates Advertising Pte Ltd.

Life's hard without Sofsil. / ソフシルがない人生はハードだ。

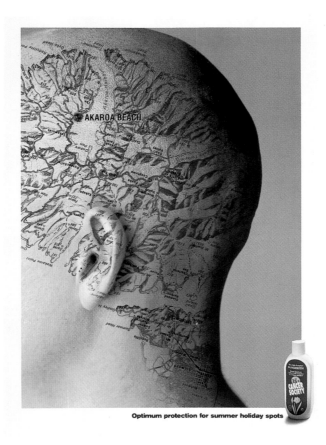

Optimum protection for summer holiday spots

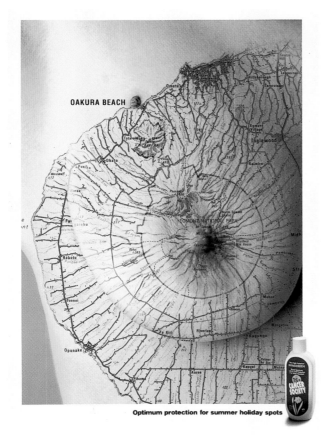

Optimum protection for summer holiday spots

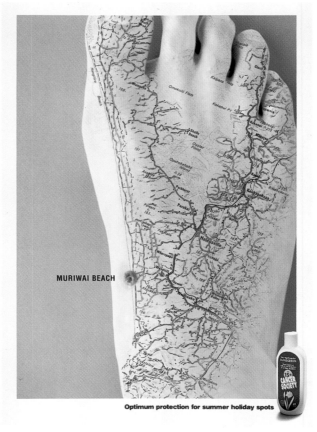

Optimum protection for summer holiday spots

Cancer Society of New Zealand
Cancer Society
ガン患者支援非営利団体
New Zealand 1997
CD: Dave Bolton
AD, D: Ben Handy
P: Sally Shapcott
CW: John O'Leary
A: Walkers Advertising

Every day, your engine is relentlessly assaulted by deposits, corrosion and wear. The best defense: Shell ROTELLA® T 15W-40 heavy-duty motor oil. It keeps engines clean, reducing wear and prolonging life. So you can fight another day. Bullet-proof protection like this is why truckers choose ROTELLA T 3 to 1 over its nearest competitor. For information, visit our web site at www.shell-lubricants.com or call 1-800-851-5028.

It's not just an oil. It's a security system.

The engine protection you get from Shell ROTELLA® T 15W-40 heavy-duty motor oil is unlike any other oil. After all, ROTELLA T doesn't simply meet industry specs; it exceeds most of them. By a wide margin. So deposits, corrosion and other enemies are neutralized. It's why truckers choose ROTELLA T 3 to 1 over its nearest competitor. For a full briefing, visit our web site at www.shell-lubricants.com or call 1-800-851-5028.

It's not just an oil. It's a security system.

When deposits, wear and heat try to vandalize your engine, Shell ROTELLA® T 15W-40 sends them a not-so-subtle signal: "Don't mess with this truck." Words backed with more testing and more on-road miles than any other oil. This ferocious protection is why truckers choose ROTELLA T 3 to 1 over its nearest competitor. Check out our web site at www.shell-lubricants.com or call 1-800-851-5028 for more information.

It's not just an oil. It's a security system.

Shell Lubricants
Oil Company
石油販売
USA 1997
CD, CW: Jay Suhr
AD, D: Karen Holland
P: Graham Westmoreland
A: Ogilvy & Mather

It's not just an oil. It's a security system.
ただのオイルじゃありません。セキュリティ・システムです。

Shell ROTELLA® T 15W-40 has always been ready to rumble with the scum that sends engines to early overhauls. Now it's packing even more muscle. The next generation of ROTELLA T works harder to protect valve trains, bearings and critical parts from soot.

It helps lower operating costs, prolong engine life and prevent loss of fuel economy. It also exceeds the brutal requirements of 1998 engines. Call it total security. Visit us at www.shell-lubricants.com or call 1-800-64-LUBES. **Count on Shell**

It's not just an oil. It's a security system.

Adapt or die. It's the law of nature and the road. Shell ROTELLA® T 15W-40 has constantly evolved to protect engines from enemies. Like soot. The next generation of ROTELLA T goes further. ROTELLA T now works harder to protect valve trains, bearings and critical parts. It helps lower operating costs, prolong engine life and prevent loss of fuel economy. It also exceeds the tougher requirements of 1998 engines. The strongest always survive. See us at www.shell-lubricants.com or call 1-800-64-LUBES. **Count on Shell**

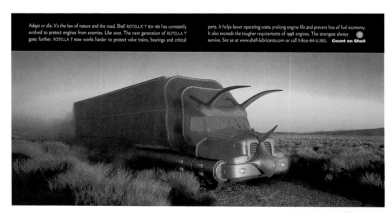

It's not just an oil. It's a security system.

Soot is an alien species on a mission to invade and destroy your engine. Neutralize it with the next generation of Shell ROTELLA® T 15W-40. Our new formulation works harder to protect valve trains, bearings and critical parts from soot. It helps lower operating costs, prolong engine life and prevent loss of fuel economy. It also exceeds the tougher requirements of 1998 engines. New ROTELLA T. It's a force you'll want with you. See us at www.shell-lubricants.com or call 1-800-64-LUBES. **Count on Shell**

It's not just an oil. It's a security system.

In the heart of Holi, India's festival of color,

our film's interimage amplifiers help

photographer Steve McCurry get extremely

saturated colors out of his pictures.

Unfortunately, they can't help him get

extremely saturated colors out of his clothes.

極彩色の水を浴びせ合うインドのホーリー祭。熱狂の中で写真家スティーブ・マッカリがとらえたイメージはコダック・フィルムによって増幅され、
鮮烈な色となって蘇る。しかし染まったシャツを蘇らせることだけはコダックにもできそうにない。

The new family of Ektachrome Elite II film delivers vibrant, pure colors across all speeds without sacrificing fleshtones. In fact, Kodak Ektachrome Elite II 100 offers the most saturated color of any amateur 100 speed slide film.

Visit us on the Internet: http://www.kodak.com

NEW EKTACHROME ELITE II

In the desert state of Rajasthan,

our film's particle filter dyes

give photographer Steve McCurry

color as you've never seen before.

Of course, you've never seen

an entire town painted blue before either.

The new family of Ektachrome Elite II film delivers vibrant, pure colors across all speeds without sacrificing fleshtones. In fact, Kodak Ektachrome Elite II 100 offers the most saturated color of any amateur 100 speed slide film.

NEW EKTACHROME ELITE II

1
2

Kodak
Camera & Film Manufacturer
精密機器・フィルム製造販売
USA 1996-97
AD: Thomas Hayo
P: Steve McCurry (1,2)
/ David Alan Harvey (3)
/ James Nachtwey (4)

1: In the heart of Holi, India's festival of color, our film's interimage amplifiers help photographer Steve McCurry get extremely saturated colors out of his pictures. Unfortunately, they can't help him get extremely saturated colors out of his clothes.
極彩色の水を浴びせ合うインドのホーリー祭。熱狂の中で写真家スティーブ・マッカリがとらえたイメージはコダック・フィルムによって増幅され、
鮮烈な色となって蘇る。しかし染まったシャツを蘇らせることだけはコダックにもできそうにない。
2: In the desert state of Rajasthan, our film's particle filter dyes give photographer Steve McCurry color as you've never seen before. Of course, you've never seen an entire town painted blue before either.
砂漠が広がるインドのラジャスターン州。写真家スティーヴ・マッカリのとらえた映像はコダック・フィルムによってかつてない繊細な色合いに仕上
がった。もちろん、町じゅうをブルーに塗ってあるというのも、かつてない光景だけれど……。

Atop the Kawah Ijen volcano,

while shooting amid clouds of poisonous

sulfuric fumes, photographer David Alan Harvey

was impressed with our film's ability

to capture extremely saturated colors.

We were impressed by how long he could hold his breath.

The new family of Ektachrome Elite II film delivers vibrant, pure colors across all speeds without sacrificing fleshtones. In fact, Kodak Ektachrome Elite II 100 offers the most saturated color of any amateur 100 speed slide film.

Visit us on the Internet: http://www.kodak.com

EKTACHROME ELITE II

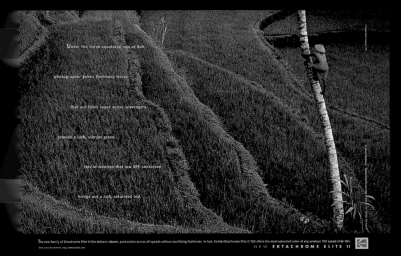

Under the harsh equatorial sun of Bali,

photographer James Nachtwey learns

that our film's super active scavengers

provide a lush, vibrant green.

Not to mention that low SPF sunscreen

brings out a rich, saturated red.

The new family of Ektachrome Elite II film delivers vibrant, pure colors across all speeds without sacrificing fleshtones. In fact, Kodak Ektachrome Elite II 100 offers the most saturated color of any amateur 100 speed slide film.

NEW **EKTACHROME ELITE II**

As the Chicago River is dyed green

to celebrate St. Patrick's Day,

photographer David Burnett appreciates

that our film's triple coating provides him

with spectacular color. The rest of Chicago would

appreciate it if they dyed it blue the other 364 days.

The new family of Ektachrome Elite II film delivers vibrant, pure colors across all speeds without sacrificing fleshtones. In fact, Kodak Ektachrome Elite II 100 offers the most saturated color of any amateur 100 speed slide film.

EKTACHROME ELITE II

3
4 5

3: Atop the Kawah Ijen volcano, while shooting amid clouds of poisonous sulfuric fumes, photographer David Alan Harvey was impressed with our film's ability to capture extremely saturated colors. We were impressed by how long he could hold his breath.
カワイジェン火山の採掘場。鼻を突く硫黄の臭いが立ちこめるなか、写真家デイヴィッド・アラン・ハーヴィーはシャッターを切った。彼はコダック・フィルムの発色の良さに思わず目を見張ったが、私たちには、あの臭いに耐えきれたことの方が驚きだった。

4: Under the harsh equatorial sun of Bali, photographer James Nachtwey learns that our film's super active scavengers provide a lush, vibrant green. Not to mention that low SPF sunscreen brings out a rich, saturated red.
太陽がじりじりと照りつける赤道直下のバリ島。写真家ジェームズ・ナハトウェイは、この豊かな緑のみずみずしさと躍動感を表現するには高性能なコダック・フィルムを使うしかないと考えた。ただし、きれいな小麦色の肌を手に入れるには、コダックより日焼けオイルの方が適している。

5: As the Chicago River is dyed green to celebrate St. Patrick's Day, photographer David Burnett appreciates that our film's triple coating provides him with spectacular color. The rest of Chicago would appreciate it if they dyed it blue the other 364 days.
聖パトリックの日を祝って緑色に染められたシカゴ川。写真家デイヴィッド・バーネットは、コダックのトリプル・コーティング技術が生み出した鮮やかな色彩に満面の笑みを浮かべた。いっそのこと、

GREASY, LIMP HAIR? SALON SELECTIVES 7+B.

OVER-STYLED, PERMED HAIR? SALON SELECTIVES 5+P.

COLOURED, FRIZZY HAIR? SALON SELECTIVES 5+M.

Elida Fabergé
Cosmetics Company
ヘア・ボディケア用品メーカー
UK 1997
CD: Dennis Lewis
AD: Tiger Savage
CW: Mark Goodwin
P: David LaChapelle
A: Bartle Bogle Hegarty Ltd.

1: Presto! Get that dak tan!
　　シマシマ黒肌ゲット！
2: Presto! Protect that white skin!
　　シマシマ白肌キープ！

Naris Cosmetics Co., Ltd.
Cosmetics Company
化粧品メーカー
Japan 1997
CD: Haruki Saburi
AD: Shin Iwasaki
D: Akiko Tsujii
I: Gogh Imaizumi
CW: Kotaro Yamazoe
A: Dai-ichi Kikaku Co., Ltd. / The Nippon Design Center Inc.

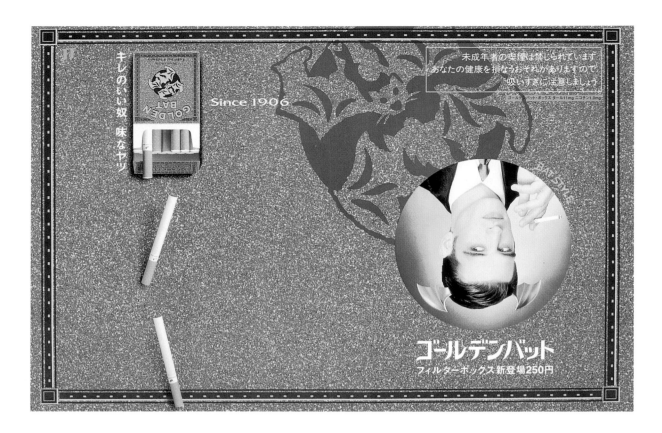

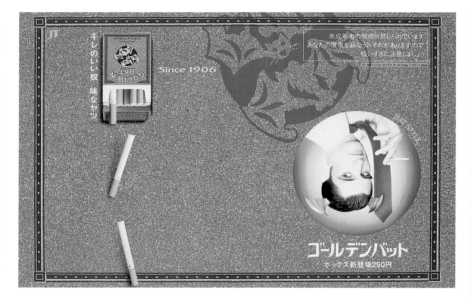

Japan Tobacco Inc.
Cigarette Manufacturer　たばこ製造販売
Japan　1997
CD: Mitsuhiro Wada
AD: Katsuo Mizuguchi / Hirosumi Takakusaki / Koichiro Toda
P: David Lachapelle
CW: Akihisa Goto
A: Dentsu Inc.

Pretty cool. Has taste.
キレのいい奴。味なヤツ

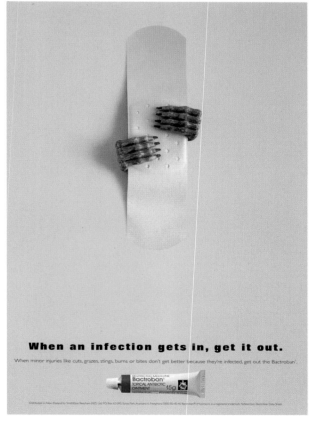

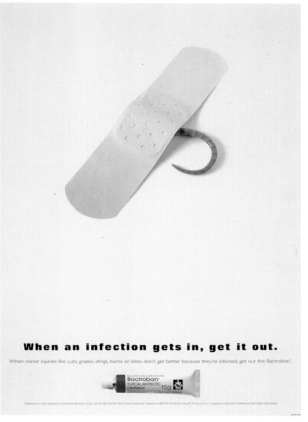

When an infection gets in, get it out. / バイ菌にやられたら、やり返せ。

Smithkline Beecham
Pharmaceutical Company
製薬会社
New Zealand 1997
CD, AD, D: Dave Brown
CD, CW: Paul White
P: Sait Akkirman
A: HKM Advertising

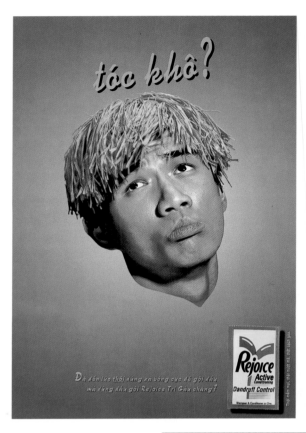

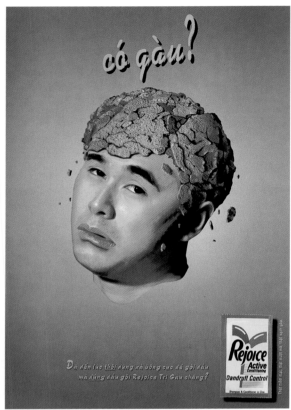

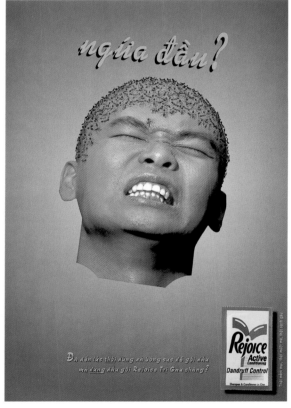

Procter and Gamble
Bath & Toiletry Products Maker
ヘアケア用品メーカー
Vietnam 1997
CD, AD: KC Arriwong
CD, CW: Richard Irvine
P: Simon Taplin / The Shooting
Gallery Singapore
A: Leo Burnett Vietnam

1: Dry hair? / 髪がバサバサ?
2: Dandruff? / フケが出る?
3: Itchy scalp? / 頭がかゆい?

WINNER OF THE OSCAR FOR PROFESSIONAL MOTION PICTURE LAMPS.

THERE'S LIGHT, AND THERE'S OSRAM. **OSRAM**

Winner of the Oscar for professional motion picture lamps.
オスカーを受賞したプロ用映画照明

Osram
Lighting Company 照明器具メーカー
Thailand 1997
CD, CW: Anurux Jansanjai
AD, D: Thirasak Tanapatanakul
P: Somporn Chotigo
I: Anuchai Secharunputong
DF: Ogilvy & Mather

Daikin Industries, Ltd.
Chemical Products Manufacturer
化学製品メーカー
Japan 1997
CD: Hiroshi Akai
AD: Ikumichi Furuhashi
D: Masashi Harada / Sayuri Motomi
P: Ichigo Sugawara
CW: Takako Nishiya
Photo PD: Hiroshi Ikeda
A: Hakuhodo Inc.,Kansai Branch

Usually, they get wet. / 普通ハ、濡レル。

And from that day on
Mr Happy always had
a big smile on his face.

THE LYNX EFFECT

Cuthbert's hose seemed
to have a life of its own.

THE LYNX EFFECT

'Stop! Stop!
I want to gobble you up!'
she shouted.

THE LYNX EFFECT

1: And from that day on Mr Happy always had a big smile on his face.
それからというもの、ミスター・ハッピーはとびっきりのスマイルを絶やしませんでした。
2: Cuthbert's hose seemed to have a life its own.
カスバートのホースは、まるで生き物みたいでした。
3: Stop! Stop! I want to gobble you up! she shouted.
「お待ち！お待ちったら！あなたを食べたいんだから！」と、おばあさんは叫びました。

Elida Fabergé
Cosmetics Company
ヘア・ボディケア用品メーカー
UK 1997
CD: Dennis Lewis
AD: Rosie Arnold
I: Roger Hargreaves（1）
/ © Gordon Murray Ltd.（2）
/ Nick Butterworth（3）
CW: Will Awdry
Typographer: Andy Bird
A: Bartle Bogle Hegarty Ltd.

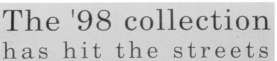

Ikea España, AB
Furniture Manufacturer
家具製造販売
Spain 1997
CD: Pedro Soler / Enrique Astuy / Delfin Martin
AD: Jorge Amich
P: David Levin
CW: Juan Carlos Salas
A: Delvico Bates, S. A.

The '98 collection has hit the streets. / '98 コレクション、ストリートを急襲。

1
2 3

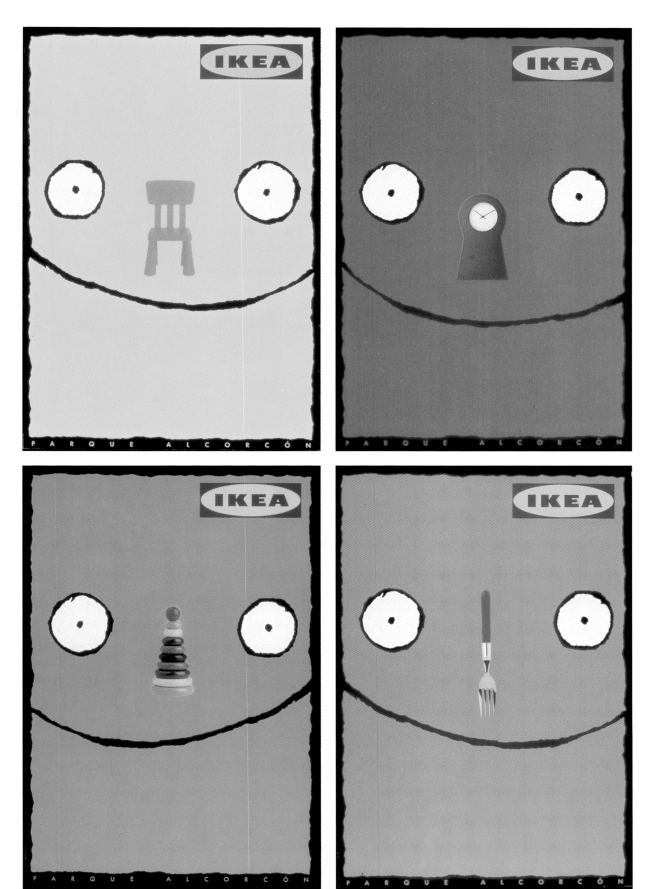

Ikea España, AB
Furniture Manufacturer
家具製造販売
Spain 1997
CD: Pedro Soler / Enrique Astuy / Delfin Martin
AD: Jorge Amich
P: David Levin
CW: Juan Carlos Salas
A: Delvico Bates, S. A.

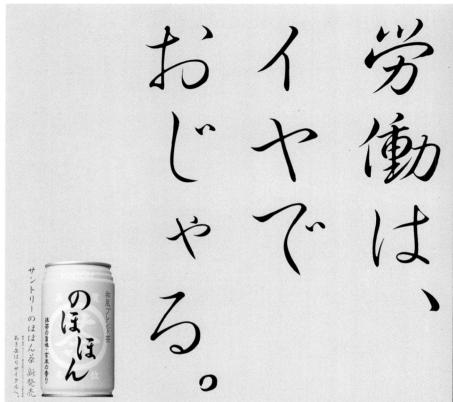

Suntory Ltd.
Beverage Maker
飲料製造販売
Japan 1998
CD, CW: Yoshiyasu Fujita
AD: Yoshihiro Kobayashi
D: Kazuma Mashima
P: Yoshihiko Ueda
DF: Kobayashi Direction Inc.

1: Work does not agree with us. / 労働は、イヤでおじゃる。
2: When the world tires you. / 世の中に、疲れたら。

渇きにくわしい飲料があります。　　大塚製薬

HUMAN WATER

飲料には、味以外にも違いがあります。たとえば、あなたはス
ポーツの後もカラダに負担をかけていませんか？ポカリスエット
なら、体内の水分に近いイオンバランスだから、吸収がスムーズ。
飲料を選ぶことが、カラダをケアすることにもなるんですね。
（スポーツの後）必要な水分と電解質。

REFRESHMENT WATER
POCARI SWEAT

あなたをサポートするNUTRACEUTICALSの大塚製薬から。
ニュートラシューティカルズ

渇きにくわしい飲料があります。　　大塚製薬

HUMAN WATER

ぐっすり眠ることは、たっぷり汗をかくことでもある。目
覚めた時のあの渇きは、カラダが水分を欲しがっている
サインなんですね。そこで、体内の水分に近いからすばやく
吸収できるポカリスエット。1分でも惜しい朝なんですから。
（目覚めた時）必要な水分と電解質。

REFRESHMENT WATER
POCARI SWEAT

あなたをサポートするNUTRACEUTICALSの大塚製薬から。
ニュートラシューティカルズ

There's one drink that knows about thirst. / 渇きにくわしい飲料があります。

Otsuka Pharmaceutical Co., Ltd.
Beverage Maker
飲料製造販売
Japan 1998
CD: Yasuyuki Kawano
AD: Jun Yoshihara
CW: Makoto Tsunoda / Hiromasa Kawana

1: **Suntory Ltd.**
Beverage Maker
飲料製造販売
Japan 1998
CD, CW: Yasuhiko Sakura
CD: Noboru Kimura
AD, D: Junichi Kojima
P: Goro Arizona
A: Sun-Ad Co., Ltd.

2,4,5,6,8: **Suntory Ltd.**
Beverage Maker
飲料製造販売
Japan 1995-96
CD: Takashi Ando / Noboru Kimura
AD, D: Junichi Kojima
P: Kazuyasu Hagane
CW: Yasuhiko Sakura
A: Sun-Ad Co., Ltd.

3,7,9: **Suntory Ltd.**
Beverage Maker
飲料製造販売
Japan 1995
CD, CW: Yasuhiko Sakura
CD: Noboru Kimura
AD, D: Junichi Kojima
P: Kazuyasu Hagane
A: Sun-Ad Co., Ltd.

1: Tastes great, baby.
うまいぜベイビー
2~9: Love is everything.
愛だろ、愛っ。

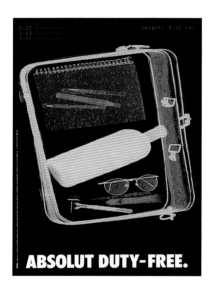

The Absolut Company
Wine & Spirits producer
酒造販売
France 1998
CD: Christophe Coffre / Nicolas Taubes
AD: Bénédicte Potel (1,2,3,5,6,7,8) / Douglas Buge (4)
CW: Thierry Lebec (1,2,3,5,6,7,8) / Vincent Detre (4)
P: Alex Chollet (4) / Vincent Dixon (6) / Graham Ford (8)
DF: TBWA Paris Advertising

1 2
3 4

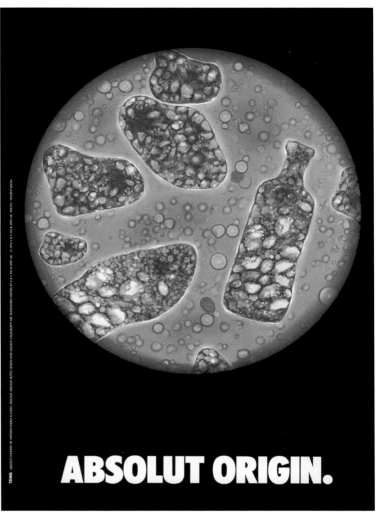

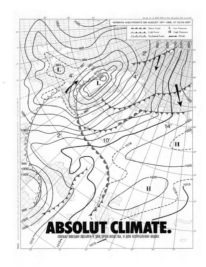

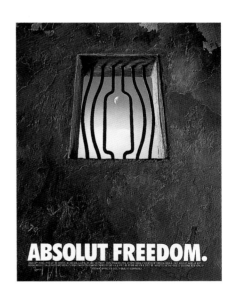

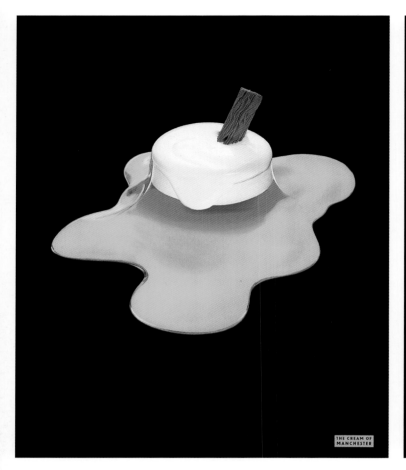

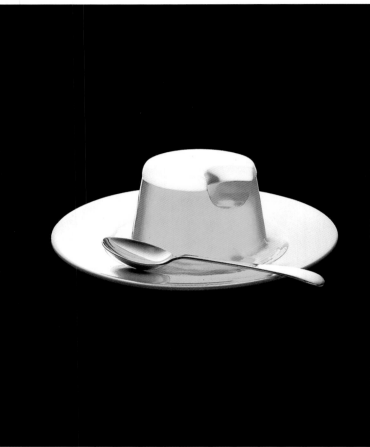

Whitbread Beer Company
Brewery Company
酒造販売
UK 1997
CD: Bruce Crouch / Graham Watson
AD: Simon Robinson
CW: Jo Moore
P: David Gill
Model Maker: Gavin Lindsey
A: Bartle Bogle Hegarty Ltd.

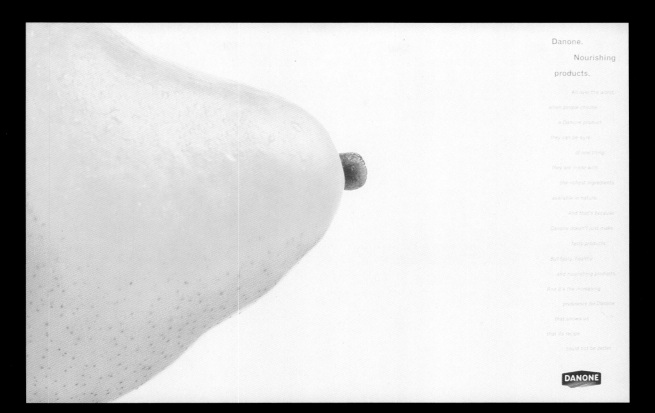

Danone
Food Manufacturer
食品製造販売
Brazil 1997
CD: Alexandre Gama
AD: Rodrigo Butori
P: Ricardo De Vicq
CW: Rita Corradi
A: Young & Rubicam Brasil

L'ABUS D'ALCOOL EST DANGEREUX POUR LA SANTÉ, CONSOMMEZ AVEC MODÉRATION.

L'ABUS D'ALCOOL EST DANGEREUX POUR LA SANTÉ, CONSOMMEZ AVEC MODÉRATION.

L'ABUS D'ALCOOL EST DANGEREUX POUR LA SANTÉ, CONSOMMEZ AVEC MODÉRATION.

Corona
Brewery Company
酒造販売
France 1997
CD: Gérard Jean
AD: Thierry Fèvre
P: Paul Goirand
CW: Loïc Froger
A: Jean & Montmarin

L'ABUS D'ALCOOL EST DANGEREUX POUR LA SANTÉ, CONSOMMEZ AVEC MODÉRATION.

L'ABUS D'ALCOOL EST DANGEREUX POUR LA SANTÉ, CONSOMMEZ AVEC MODÉRATION.

L'ABUS D'ALCOOL EST DANGEREUX POUR LA SANTÉ, CONSOMMEZ AVEC MODÉRATION.

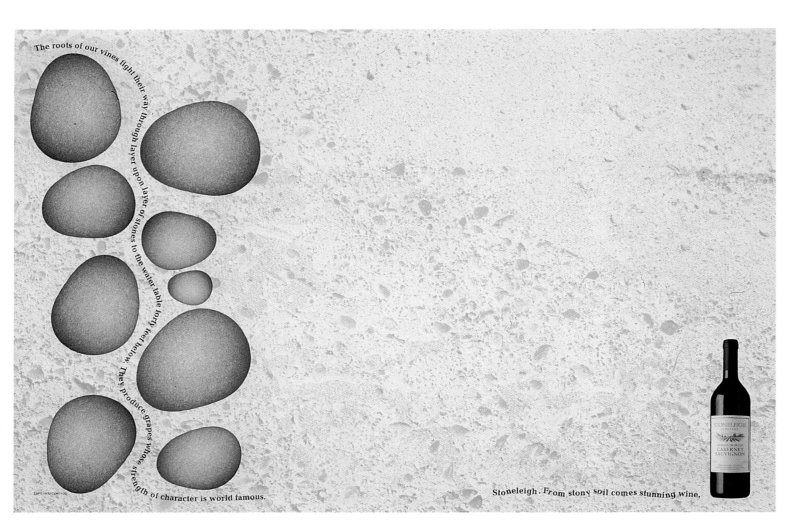

Stoneleigh. From stony soil comes stunning wine.

Corbans Wine
Wine Producer
酒造販売
New Zealand 1997
CD, AD, D: Dave Brown
CD, CW: Paul White
P: Warren Payne
A: HKM Advertising

1: The roots of our vines fight their way through layer upon layer of stones to the water table forty feet below. They produce grapes whose strength of character is world famous.
　私たちのブドウは分厚い石の層をかいくぐって40フィートも下の地下水まで根をおろします。世界有数の力強いブドウが実るのは石のおかげなのです。

2: In the heat of the day stones warm up. In the cool of the evening their warmth heats the vines. Another reason why our wines shine in competitions all over the world.
　日中、太陽エネルギーを吸収した石が、気温の下がる夜間に熱を放出し、ブドウの生育を促します。私たちのワインが数ある銘柄のなかでひときわ輝いているのは石のおかげなのです。

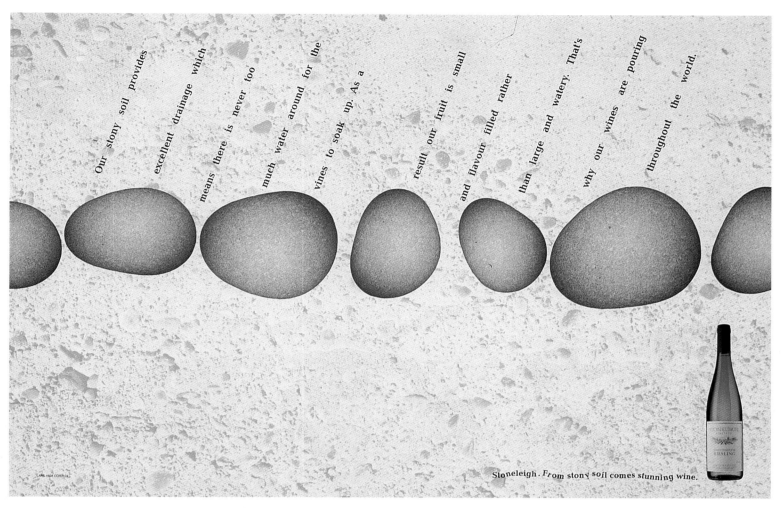

Our stony soil provides excellent drainage which means there is never too much water around for the vines to soak up. As a result our fruit is small and flavour filled rather than large and watery. That's why our wines are pouring throughout the world.

Stoneleigh. From stony soil comes stunning wine.

Stony soil creates havoc for farmers but heaven for wine makers. That's why we planted our vineyard in the finest sauvignon blanc region in the world.

Stoneleigh. From stony soil comes stunning wine.

We can't get blood out of a stone but we do get a hint of gooseberry, a touch of asparagus, a whiff of grass and a dash of nettles. That's how we make some of the finest sauvignon blanc in the world.

Stoneleigh. From stony soil comes stunning wine.

3
4 5

3: Our stony soil provides excellent drainage which means there is never too much water around for the vines to soak up. As a result our fruit is small and flavour filled rather than large and watery. That's why our wines are pouring throughout the world.
石の多い土壌は水はけがよく、ブドウの木に余計な水分を与えません。その結果、香りや味の凝縮された小粒のブドウが実ります。私たちのワインが世界じゅうで愛されているのは石のおかげなのです。
4: Stony soil creates havoc for farmers but heaven for wine makers. That's why we planted our vineyard in the finest sauvignon blanc region in the world.
石の多い土壌は農民にとっては地獄ですが、ワイン職人にとっては天国です。私たちのブドウ園で世界一のソービニヨン・ブランが育つのも石のおかげなのです。
5: We can't get blood out of a stone but we do get a hint of gooseberry, a touch of asparagus, a whiff of grass and a dash of nettles. That's how we make some of the finest sauvignon blanc in the world.
石の多い土壌で育つブドウには、スグリやアスパラガスや青草や苛草のほのかな香りが加わります。最高級のソーヴィニョン・ブランと言われるのも石のおかげなのです。

Fisherman's Friend
Food Manufacturer
食品製造販売
Belgium 1996
CD: Werner Van Reck
AD, CW: Paul Popelier
P: Christian D'hoir
A: Ldv / Partners

1: Red hot sauce inflames desire. / スパイスのきいたソース、欲望の火をつける
2: Red hot sauce strikes imagination. / このソース、きいたスパイスが想像をかきたてる

Lebedyan
Food Manufacturer
食品製造販売
Russia 1998
CD: Andreev
AD, D, I: Fadeev
P: Bairak
CW: Bychkov / Morozov
A: C-Pro Production

Birba
Biscuit Maker
菓子メーカー
Spain 1997
CD: Jose Gamo
AD: Enric Aguilera
P: Super Stock / Ramon Serrano
CW: Cesar Garcia
A: Tiempo / BBDO

Troubled with chemicals? / 添加物でお困りですか？

It's quicker to swallow a Pepsi Slam. / 飲み込むなら、ペプシ・スラムの方が早いよ。

Pepsi
Beverage Maker
飲料製造販売
UK 1996
CD: David Abbott
AD: Greg Martin
P: Malcolm Venville
CW: Pat Domerty
A: Abbott Mead Vickers・BBDO Ltd.

PERRIER
Mineral Water Bottler
飲料製造販売
Australia 1997
CD: John Nankeruis
AD: Jim Sanders
P: Simon Harsent
CW: Edward Richards
A: Foote, Cone & Belding Sydney Pty Ltd.

Varma, S. A.
Distiller
酒造販売
Spain 1997
CD: Pedro Soler / Enrique Astuy / Delfin Martin
AD: Jorge Amich
P: Jesus Chamizo
CW: Juan Carlos Salas
A: Delvico Bates. S. A.

Kibon
Food Manufacturer
食品製造販売
Brazil 1996
CD: Alexandre Gama
AD: Rodrigo Butori
P: Marquinhos
I: Brasilio Matsumoto
CW: Isabella Paulelli

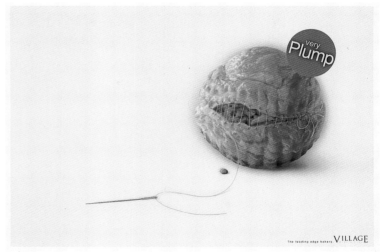

Village Bake'n Cake
Bakery
ベーカリー
Thailand 1997
CD: Anurux Jansanjai
AD, D: Thirasak Tanapatanakul
P: Somporn Chotigo
I: Anuchai Secharunputong
CW: Chris Lapsley / Saipet Na Ubon
A: Ogilvy & Mather

Bob gets baffled watching Junior Masterchef, thinks Risotto is an Italian footballer and once mistook a fish knife for a D.I.Y. tool.

He made this in 10 minutes.

(Bob's) SHELLFISH STIR FRY
Onion, garlic + ginger — fry for 1 min.
Packet of stirfry VEG — another 3 mins.
Add mix of SHELLFISH (prawns, scallops, mussels) — whatever.
Don't overcook!
+ WINE!

FISH. Go on, surprise yourself.

Val is into French cuisine, Dutch cheeses, Italian gnocchi and Spanish paella. But every now and again she gets patriotic.

FISH. Go on, surprise yourself.

Jim thinks kitchens are only good for finding people at parties and is on first name terms with the staff of all his local Take-Aways.

He knocked this out in 15 minutes.

Fast Fishy Pizza
4 tbl. spoons burger relish onto ½ baked bread
Smoked mackerel — flaked
Grate mozzarella
10 mins in oven (v. hot)

FISH. Go on, surprise yourself.

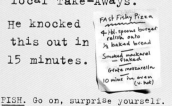

Seafish Industry Authority
Seafish Authority
漁業協同組合
UK 1997
AD, Typographer: Shaun Stoker
P: Martin Thompson / Victor Albrow
CW: Rich Lee
Media: Gillian Cairney
Production: Grant Byrne
A: Faulds Advertising

1: Bob gets baffled watching Junior Masterchef, thinks Risotto is an Italian footballer and once mistook a fish knife for a D.I.Y. tool. He made this in 10 minutes.
ボブは子供向けの料理番組をみてもさっぱりわからない。「リゾット」はイタリアのサッカー選手の名前だと思っているし、魚用のナイフを大工道具と間違えたこともある。そんな彼でも１０分でできたのがこれ。

2: Val is into French cuisine, Dutch cheeses, Italian gnocchi and Spanish paella. But every now and again she gets patriotic.
バルはフランス料理が大好き。オランダのチーズ、イタリアのニョッキ、スペインのパエリアにも凝っている。でも、やっぱりイギリス人。時々どうしても食べたくなるのがこれ。

3: Jim thinks kitchens are only good for finding people at parties and is on first name terms with the staff of all his local Take-Aways. He knocked this out in 15 minutes.
ジムはキッチンと言えばホームパーティで話し相手を見つける場所だと思っている。近所のテイクアウトの店ではすっかり顔なじみだ。そんな彼でも15分でできちゃったのがこれ。

Bev hated home economics at school, has never bought a cookery book in her life and fast-forwards through the recipe pages of women's magazines.

She made this for the family in around 10 minutes.

Mexican Fish Pie
1. Stick fish in a 2pt dish.
2. Pour on salsa & microwave – on high for 2 mins.
3. Add beans & top with – mashed spuds & tortilla chips
4. Cook on high for 3 mins.

<u>FISH</u>. Go on, surprise yourself.

EUROPEAN COMMUNITY
Financial Instrument
for Fisheries Guidance

SEAFISH

Tom is totally committed to developing his skills as a top cordon bleu chef. But occasionally he likes to take time off.

FOOD ORDER
DAY OFF
Haircut
Bank
Cinema?
Frozen Cod
Steaks

<u>FISH</u>. Go on, surprise yourself.

SEAFISH

Liz likes her vegetables al dente, her salads à la Provençale, her pasta alla puttanesca and her fish fingers in ketchup.

MEMO
COUSCOUS
BORLOTTI BEANS
FLAT LEAF PARSLEY
FISH FINGERS

<u>FISH</u>. Go on, surprise yourself.

SEAFISH

4
5 6

4: Bev hated home economics at school, has never bought a cookery book in her life and fast-forwards through the recipe pages of women's magazines. She made this for the family in around 10 minutes.
ベブは家庭科が大嫌いだった。料理の本は一度も買ったことがないし、雑誌を読むときもレシピのコーナーはとばしてしまう。そんな彼女が家族のために10分で作ったのがこれ。

5: Tom is totally committed to developing his skills as a top cordon bleu chef. But occasionally he likes to take time off.
トムは一流シェフを目指して修行に励む毎日。でも、たまの休みくらいは手を抜きたい。そんな時にはこれ。

6: Liz likes her vegetables al dente, her salads à la provençale, her pasta alla puttanesca and her fish fingers in ketchup.
リズは野菜やパスタの茹で具合にうるさい。プロヴァンス風サラダもプッタネスカスパゲティもアルデンテでなければダメ。もちろんフィッシュフライはケチャップつきだ。

Or try Diet Form.

Diet Form.
Less calories.
Same taste.

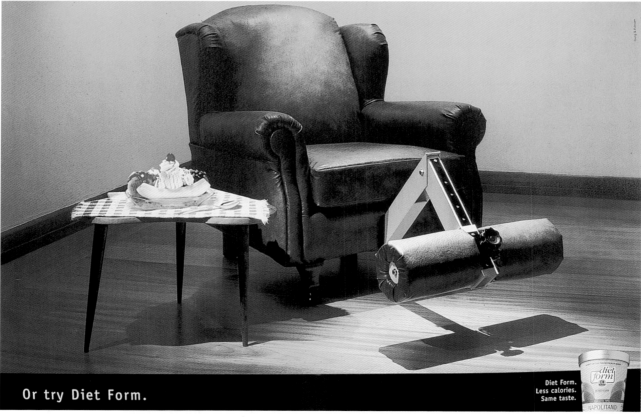

Or try Diet Form.

Diet Form.
Less calories.
Same taste.

Kibon
Food Manufacturer
食品製造販売
Brazil 1998
CD, CW: Alexandre Gama
AD: Cassiano Borges
P: Mauricio Nahas / Miro
A: Young & Rubicam Brasil

Or try Diet Form.
それともダイエット・フォームを試しますか

Other Papers still have their place. / 他の新聞にも使い道はある。

Sports Only
Newspaper
新聞社
Canada 1997
CD: Darrel Shee
AD: Jeffrey Hilts
P: Robert Earnest
CW: Eric Howling
A: Bryant Fulton & Shee

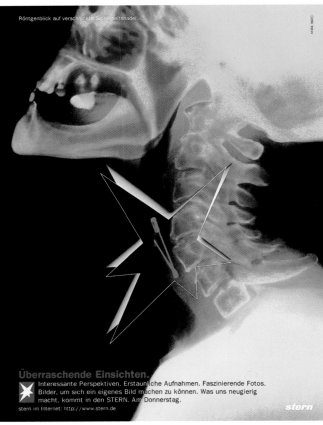

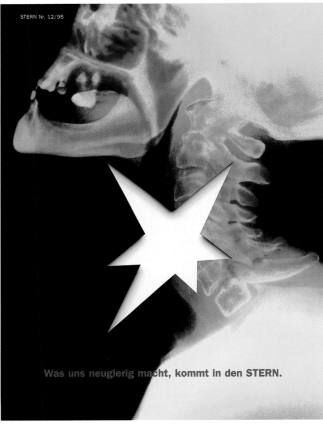

Gruner + Jahr AG & Co.1
Publisher
出版社
Germany 1997
CD: Beat Naegeu / Wolfgang Sasse
AD: Juergen Florenz / René Wolf
CW: Kai Flemming
A: KNSK, BBDO Werbeagentur GmbH, GWA

1: What's happening in the world is in STERN. Current events.
Photos that shock us. Pictures that move us. Reports that take hold and create talking points.
世界で今起っていること、それはSTERNに掲載される。今現に起っている事件。
☆驚世の写真。激動する映像。頭から振り払うことのできない、論議を呼び起すルポルタージュ。
2: What makes us curious is in STERN. Surprising insights.
Interesting perspectives. Incredible images. Fascinating photographs. Pictures for you to form your own impressions.
我々の好奇心をかきたてるもの、それはSTERNに掲載される。驚くべき見識。
☆興味深い展望。驚愕すべき撮影。魅惑する写真。実像をまざまざと想起させる映像。

3: What's surprising is in STERN. Research with no respect. We are no court correspondents.
☆We describe and analyse the most significant and noteworthy news from politics and business.
思いもかけず驚くべきこと、それはSTERNに掲載される。遠慮容赦ない取材。
☆我々が提供するのは御用報道ではない。我々は政治経済の分野から最も重要で、最も注目すべき問題を、大胆に、また中立的立場で議論し分析する。

4: What's to be discovered is in STERN. New insights.
☆The world we live in. As seen by the world's best photographers. Pictures for you to form your own impressions.
暴かれるべきもの。それはSTERNに掲載される。
☆我々が生きている世界。世界一流の写真家の視点から。実像をまざまざと想起させる映像。

5: What turns us on is in STERN. Erotic moments.
☆Beautiful pictures that seduce us. Sensual pictures from the world's best photographers. Surprising photos that tell stories.
我々の気をそそるもの、それはSTERNに掲載される。エロティックな瞬間。
☆我々を誘惑する素晴らしく美しい撮影。世界一流の写真家による官能的映像。歴史を語る驚くべき写真。

3
4
5

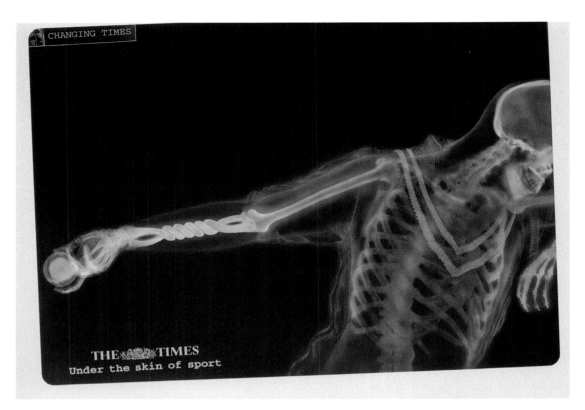

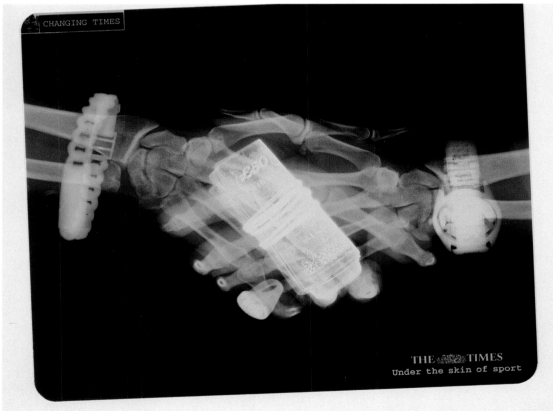

The Times
Newspaper 新聞社
UK 1997
CD: Robert Campbell / Mark Roalfe
AD: Graham Storey
P: Tim O'Sullivan
CW: Phil Cockrell
A: Rainey, Kelly, Campbell, Roalfe

Under the skin of sport. / スポーツをひと皮むけば

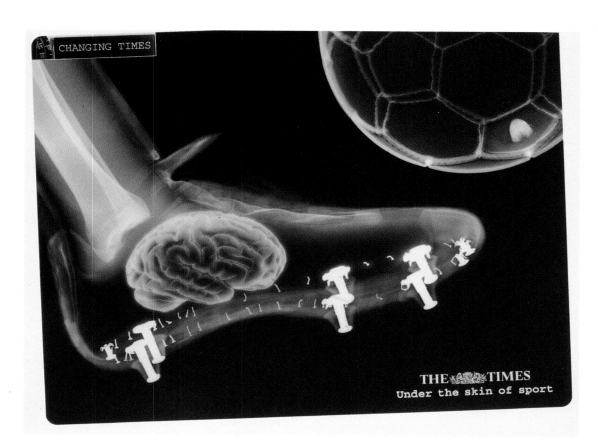

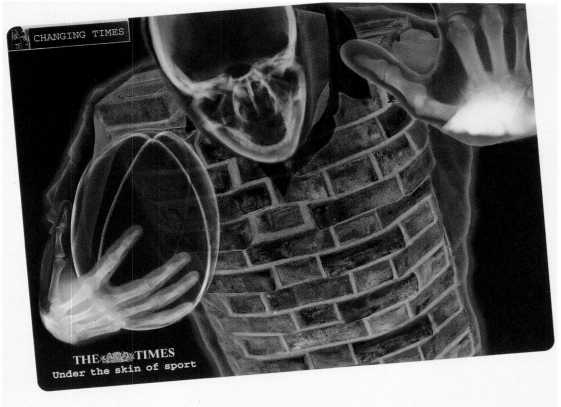

BÅDE OG...
Radio Station
ラジオ局
Norway 1998
AD: Tom Aanensen
P: Per Heimly
CW: Fred Hauge
A: Bold Reklamebyrå Ås

1: It's a good idea. But how about following the examples of Barble, Bogle, and Blubbarty ?
いい考えだ、でも少しはバルブレ、ボグレ、ブルッバーティの真似をしたら。
2: Damn it! It cannot be helped. No customers at all. My business is ruined.
チクショー、しょうがねぇな。とにかく、客が来ないんだから、商売にならない。

3: A new way of thinking is certainly wonderful, young fellow. But, almost all things have already been done by someone else long ago.
新しい考え方はたしかに素晴らしいことだ、若者よ。でも、殆どのことは、ずっと昔、だれかが既にやったことなんだ。
4: Young fellow, it is also important to think according to a certain concept.
若者よ、コンセプトに従って考えることも大切だよ。

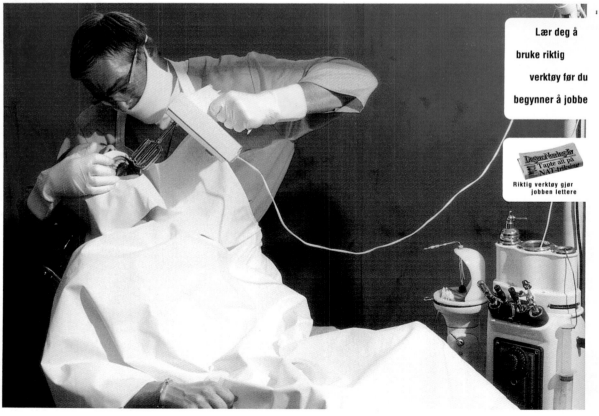

Dagens Næringsliv
Newspaper
新聞社
Norway 1998
AD: Øivind Lie
P: Johan Wildhagen
CW: Ragnar Roksvåg
A: Bold Reklamebyrå As

1: Use a right tool from the stage of learning at school.
　学校で勉強している段階から、工具はきちんとしたものを使うこと。
2: Learn the right way of using tools before you start to work.
　正しい工具の使い方は、働き始める前に学ぶこと。
3,4: A proper tool helps you work easier.
　適切な工具を使うと、仕事が楽になる。

Riktig verktøy gjør jobben lettere

Riktig verktøy gjør jobben lettere

3
4

Sony Music Entertainment Inc.
Record Company
レコード会社
Japan 1995
CD, CW: Tsuyoshi Fujimoto
AD, D: Osamu Fukushima
P: Naoki Tsuruta
A: Asatsu Inc.

The record store. A place to meet gods.
レコード屋さんは、神様たちに会える場所。

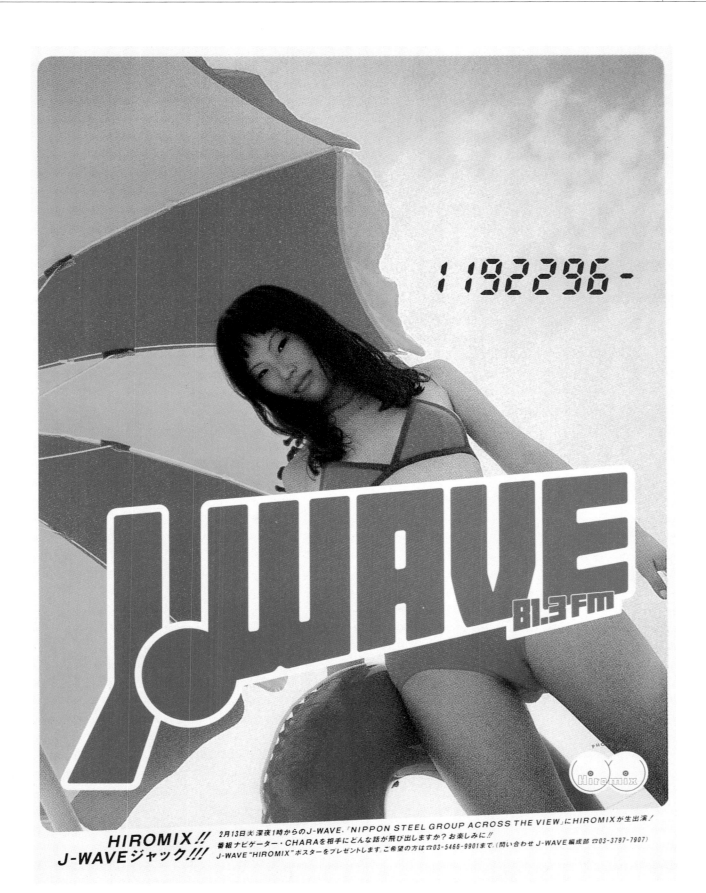

HIROMIX !!
J-WAVEジャック!!!

2月13日火深夜1時からのJ-WAVE,「NIPPON STEEL GROUP ACROSS THE VIEW」にHIROMIXが生出演！
番組ナビゲーター・CHARAを相手にどんな話が飛び出しますか？お楽しみに!!
J-WAVE "HIROMIX" ポスターをプレゼントします。ご希望の方は☎03-5466-9901まで。(問い合わせ J-WAVE編成部 ☎03-3797-7907)

J-Wave
Radio Station
ラジオ局
Japan 1996
AD, D, CW: Gugi Akiyama
P: Hiromix
PD: Yukihiko Asano
Copy Director: Ikko Seki
A: I & S Corp.

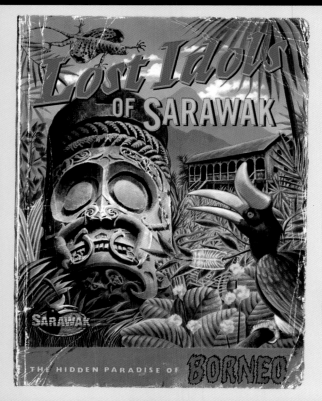

FOR 40,000 YEARS THEY'VE BEEN COMING HERE TO GET AWAY FROM IT ALL.

ARCHAEOLOGISTS tell us that the first humans to arrive in Southeast Asia chose to live in Sarawak. No one can say with any certainty why these early stone-age wanderers made for this particular corner of the region. But as you stroll through the spectacular caves of Sarawak, some so huge you could fit a handful of cathedrals in them, you can't help but wonder. Was this perhaps the first emergence 40,000 years ago of that essentially human characteristic, the desire for a more grandiose home?

Of course, we shall never know. But whatever their reasons, they certainly started something of a trend. Over the years, this charmed land on the northwestern edge of Borneo has been the essential port of call for generations of enterprising travellers. In the 6th century, the Chinese came in search of the finest edible bird's nest. In the 8th century, Arabian princes sent their emissaries to collect the world's best camphor.

And in the 16th century, the bedraggled remnants of Magellan's crew arrived. After two years at sea, during which hunger had forced them to eat the leather off the masts, they finally put Borneo on the European map. Not long after that, a host of would-be Indiana Joneses set sail to make their fortune. For some – like Rajah Brooke who established the dynasty of the White Rajahs – the dream came true. But others simply found themselves enslaved by pirates, and sold off in the classified ads section of the Java Courant.

Access to Sarawak has improved a lot since the days of sailing ships and pirates. It now takes just over an hour from Singapore. Nonetheless, for the traveller looking for something more rewarding than a simple beach holiday, Sarawak still possesses riches beyond measure. Not gold and diamonds – although there are plentiful deposits – but the sort of riches which screech and squawk. The gibbons which sing in the trees every dawn, for example. Or the bearded pigs which stand on their hind legs to reach the fruit up in the cocoa trees. Trek, or climb or just simply wander in this country-sized botanic garden and you can discover a fresh wonder at every turn. A new variety of orchid, perhaps. Or you might even catch a glimpse of something more elusive still. The ancient Penan nomads – some of the world's last hunter-gatherers – slipping silently through the trees with their blowpipes and poison-tipped darts.

For more information and a brochure about holidays in Sarawak, please contact the Sarawak Tourism Board on tel: 60 82 423600 or fax: 60 82 416700 or visit our website at http://www.sarawak.gov.my/stb

Early seafarers faced numerous perils; typhoons could appear out of nowhere, and pirates swarmed off the shores of Borneo like hornets.

A rare example of a man who sailed away to seek his fortune and found it. James Brooke, the first of the White Rajahs.

150 years ago, a young warrior's marriage prospects were considerably enhanced if he possessed a good collection of heads.

SAR-9703

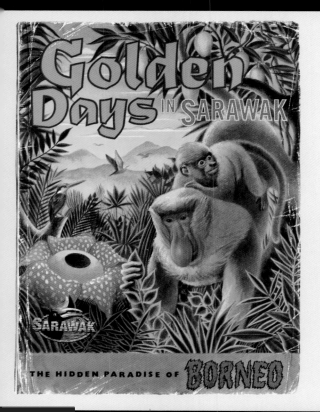

THEY SAY THAT, IN THIS LAND, CHILDREN NEVER FALL ASLEEP IN A BIOLOGY LESSON.

THE YOUNG couple first heard the phrase from another traveller, a backpacker, who shared the boat with them as they travelled up the Rajang River. He was heading deep into the rainforest in search of the Penan, some of the world's last true hunter-gatherers. And they had chosen to stop off and sample the hospitality of the Iban longhouses.

Whether a piece of ancient tribal wisdom or just the happy invention of the backpacker, the truth of the words will echo through your thoughts repeatedly as you journey through Sarawak. Located on the northwestern edge of Borneo and just over an hour from Singapore, the country resembles nothing so much as one huge botanic garden. A world where tiny deer the size of cats share the forest with bearded pigs. Where orang-utans swinging through the trees find themselves overtaken by squirrels gliding past on wings of fur. And where countless other surprises await you at every turn. Such as the world's biggest flower, the astonishing Rafflesia plant, which pops open with a gigantic orange bloom measuring over a metre across.

It is unlikely, alas, that the backpacker managed to find the Penan. The ancient rainforest stretches for many thousands of square kilometres, and these forest nomads, with their blowpipes and poison-tipped darts, slip through the trees with the stealth of a leopard. But all the other natural wonders can be enjoyed with ease.

Whether, in fact, you choose to trek, climb, cycle or simply wander, you will find every day in Sarawak is an adventure. Even those spent in the tranquil town of Kuching, where forays into the rainforest begin and end. Sit at a waterfront coffeeshop sipping the strong Bornean coffee and you will be following in the footsteps of countless generations of travellers. Novelists like Joseph Conrad and Somerset Maugham. Pirates and Malay princes. Headhunters and fortune seekers. And even – as if to give Sarawak the official seal of approval as a land of thrills – the legendary cartoon hero Tintin once paid a visit. Yes, as you inhale the incense-scented breeze from the river, you will be forced to agree.

The school children of Sarawak are indeed fortunate. Where else in the world can you study local history by reading Tintin?

For more information and a brochure about holidays in Sarawak, please contact the Sarawak Tourism Board in one of the following ways: tel: 60 82 423600 or fax: 60 82 416700 or visit our website at http://www.sarawak.gov.my/stb

In a world filled with wonders, few are more touching than an encounter with a gentle orang-utan.

This funeral pole is typical of the artistry of native carvers. Most longhouses have carved figures at the entrance to ward off stray spirits.

Flying lizards glide on wings formed from a membrane of stretched skin. Some frogs and snakes defy gravity in a similar fashion.

The Penan nomads cultivate wild sago and hunt for small game, using darts tipped with the poisonous sap of the ipoh tree.

m Board
rism Board
観光局
pore 1997
Khai Meng
Ian Batey
David Chin
olm Pryce
Singapore

1
2
3
4

Rainbow's End IN SARAWAK
THE HIDDEN PARADISE OF BORNEO

THE IBAN MAIDENS WERE TOTALLY MERCILESS. "NO PHOTOS," THEY LAUGHED, "UNLESS YOU DANCE THE NGAJAT!"

DRUM BEATS thudded out into the hot tropical night. Tribal gongs clanged. And the Iban girls, silver coins jingling on their tribal dresses, stepped forward with smiles of delight. For the honeymoon couple, there was now no possibility of escape. They were going to have to dance the *ngajat*.

But then no one comes to Sarawak just to sunbathe (even though the soft white sands, criss-crossed with turtle footprints, are ideal for this pastime). Instead, the wise traveller casts his fate into a boat and follows the call of the mighty Rajang River.

Over the years the river and its latticework of tributaries has borne countless generations of adventure-seekers – from traders and headhunters, to pirates and the odd novelist – deep into the ancient jungle.

Through a botanic wonderland where proboscis monkeys squeal from the trees and lizards and frogs glide down from the skies. And where today you may stare into the eyes of an orang-utan, and be forever haunted by the feeling of how human he seems. Just as he, too, will be perplexed at how much like an orang-utan you are.

Yes, a visit to this enchanted land on the northwestern edge of Borneo is proof that it is still possible to find adventure in this increasingly sanitised world. It no longer takes a week's sailing from Singapore by schooner, you

can get here in little over an hour. But the essential feeling of entering a different world is still the same. Especially at dusk when you break your journey upriver and sample the legendary hospitality of the longhouses – the

In a timeless natural cycle, green turtles return every year to the shores of their birthplace in northern Borneo to lay eggs.

ancestral homes of the tribes which are strung out along the river like beads on a string. Here you may find, hidden away in the cobwebbed corners, the accumulated baggage of Sarawak's fascinating past: ancient Chinese jars; an antique brass cannon; a faded picture of Queen Victoria; and, occasionally hanging from the rafters, a dusty chandelier of skulls.

The rule of the longhouse is simple and it hasn't changed since the days when Joseph Conrad and Somerset Maugham wrote their stories here by the flickering light of the fire-flies. Guests, it is felt, should always make a little contribution to the entertainment. So when the gongs strike up, push aside the remains of your chicken-in-bamboo supper, take one last sip from the heady *tuak* rice wine, and dance the *ngajat* for all you're worth.

For more information and a brochure about holidays in Sarawak, please contact the Sarawak Tourism Board in one of the following ways: tel: 60 82 423600 or fax: 60 82 416700 or visit our website at http://www.sarawak.gov.my/stb

Warrior from the rainforest, as seen through 19th century eyes. Such romanticised images were typical of early western accounts of Sarawak.

Squirrels, lizards, frogs and even snakes are some of the normally earthbound animals in the rainforest that glide through the air on flaps of stretched skin.

SAR-9701

THE LEOPARD SANG IN SARAWAK
THE HIDDEN PARADISE OF BORNEO

ARE THERE REALLY PLANTS OUT THERE IN THE RAINFOREST WHICH EAT ANIMALS?

THE IDEA had seemed just too far-fetched when Asun the guide first mentioned it to the young honeymoon couple. Then when he added that he would also be taking them to look for squirrels which flew and macaques which dived for crabs, they knew he had to be pulling their legs. (This was before he had even mentioned pigs sporting beards.)

But he was serious. Flying frogs and squirrels are actually some of the saner things you could encounter on a visit to Sarawak. Perched on the northwestern edge of Borneo just

The stream of bats leaving the Deer Cave at dusk takes more than an hour to pass.

over an hour from Singapore, and covered with an expanse of primeval rainforest bigger than Austria, it's one of the last great lands of adventure left in this world.

Day begins here not with the commonplace crowing of the cockerel, but the haunting sound of gibbons in the treetops, singing their hymn to the dawn. Among the foliage, you may see tiny deer the size of cats. Or hear, if you listen very carefully, the microscopic too-wit too-woo of an owl smaller than a butterfly. And nearby, find butterflies so big, that a Victorian naturalist – in one of his less sober moments – shot a specimen with his rifle.

The same Victorian naturalist complained that his sense of wonder almost died from overwork during

A Goliath among flowers, the Rafflesia is the world's largest flowering plant with a bloom that can measure up to a metre across.

Assassins of the plant world, pitcher plants survive in poor quality soil by trapping unwary flies and slowly digesting them.

his stay in Sarawak. You, too, may begin to doubt the evidence of your senses as you wander through caves bigger than cathedrals and trek across some of the oldest rainforest in the world. Or even encounter the famous carnivorous pitcher plants which trap flies in their saxophone shaped leaves and then digest

The local name for proboscis monkey means 'dutchman' – a mischievous reference to the impressive noses of the early European visitors.

them in a reservoir of corrosive fluid. Some varieties in Borneo grow so big that even drowned rats have been reported dissolving in the enzyme soup.

Day ends just as magically as it begins. Armies of fire-flies begin to flicker, phosphorescent mushrooms glow, and from the mouth of the great Deer Cave in Mulu National Park a river of bats emerges. Not just hundreds of bats. Nor even thousands. But a never-ending spiral of millions that will momentarily eclipse the Sarawak moon and consume three tons of insects before dawn.

Throughout the hot night they forage, over the dark canopy of the rainforest, over the gibbons sleeping in the trees, and over those strange pitcher plants with which they share the same taste in insects.

For more information and a brochure about holidays in Sarawak, please contact the Sarawak Tourism Board in one of the following ways: tel: 60 82 423600 or fax: 60 82 416700 or visit our website at http://www.sarawak.goc.my/stb

SAR-9702

Tokyo Dome Corp.
Amusement Park
遊園地
Japan 1996
CD: Katsuhiro Otomo
AD, D: Gugi Akiyama
CW: Ikko Seki
Collage: Tadashi Saito
PD: Shinichi Yamashita / Eiko Tanaka
A: I & S Corp.

1: It's about time to get up...
そろそろ起きてもいいかな

1: **Oo Records Inc.**
Record Company
レコード会社
Japan 1995
CD, CW: Tsuyoshi Fujimoto
AD, D: Osamu Fukushima
P: Kazuyoshi Hagane
A: Asatsu Inc.

2: **Hakuhodo Inc.**
Advertising Agency
広告代理店
Japan 1997
CD: Satoshi Suzuki
AD: Kashiwa Sato
D: Jun Kamata / Akifumi Nishiura / Tadashi Yui
I: Tomoe Eno
A: Hakuhodo Inc.

Jidaimura
Theme Park Planners
テーマパークの企画・運営
Japan 1998
CD: Hiroshi Yonemura / Hisashi Fujii
AD, D, I: Kenjiro Sano
D: Shinji Ueno
P: Hiromasa Gamou
I: Shoko Yokota / Koji Azuma
CW: Kenji Saito
Logo design: Masayoshi Nakajo
A: Hakuhodo Inc.

Queue on down.
来てちょんまげ。

Fuji Kyuko Co., Ltd.
Amusement Park
遊園地
Japan 1998
CD: Kazuo Arai
AD: Shumei Takahashi
D: Yuji Suzuki / Yutaka Sugiura
P: Hatsuhiko Okada
CW: Yuka Tsukada
DF: Ad Brain

Digi Cube
Game Maker
ゲームメーカー
Japan 1997
CD: Yoshiharu Sengoku
AD: Naonobu Nakamura
D: Tatsuya Kitabayashi
P: Luc Delahaya (color) / Donovan Wylie (monochrome)
CW: Tetsuo Ueda
PD: Taku Ito
A: Dentsu Tec Inc.

It might be adults who confuse reality with games.
現実とゲームを混同しているのは、大人かもしれない。

1: Civilization is overrated.
文明は過大評価されている。
2: You haven't lived until you've crossed wakes with a duck.
水鳥たちと水面を分かち合わなければ、「生きる」ことの本当の意味はわからない。
3: Experience the incredible rush of moving at three miles per hour.
時速5キロの快感を味わってみないか。

Walden Paddlers
Recreational Goods Maker
レジャー用品メーカー
USA 1997
CD, AD: Rob Rich
CD: Steve Bautista
P: Jim Flynn
CW: Eivind Ueland
A: Ingalls

Thai Airways International PCL
Airline
航空会社
Japan 1996(1),97(2)
CD: Koichi Kano
CD, CW: Konosuke Kamitani
AD: Yoshihisa Suzuki
D: Kyoichi Iwakuni
P: Hatsuhiko Okada
CW: Naoto Odate
DF: Dentsu Inc. / Taki Corp.
A: Dentsu Inc.

Thai love you / Thai. Go while you're young.
タイラブユー / タイは、若いうちに行け

Oslo Gay and Lesbian Festival
ゲイ＆レズビアンフェスティバル協会
Norway 1997-98
AD: Anne Gravingen
P: Alf Børjesson
I: Bjørn Brockmann
CW: Benoik Romstad
A: Bates Camp

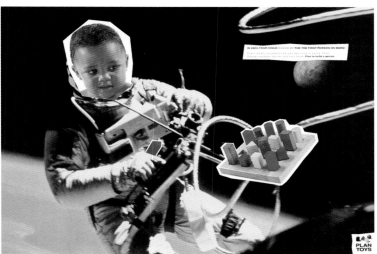

1: By 2030, your child could have designed a 280 storey tower in the middle of Manhattan! Tomorrow's success stories are still little children today. Choose intelligent toys to build your kid's future. Plan to build a genius.
2030年。お宅の赤ちゃんがマンハッタンのど真ん中に280階建のビルを設計するかもしれません。明日のサクセスストーリーの主人公は、今はまだ子ども。知能を育てる玩具を選んで、お子さんの未来を開く。それが天才への第一歩。

2: In 2023, your child could be the the first person on Mars! Every wildly successful person was once a young child. Choose intelligent toys for your kid's future. Plan to build a genius.
2023年。お子さんは初の火星探索に成功するかもしれません。どんな冒険者も昔はみんな子ども。お子さんの未来のために知能を育てる玩具を選びましょう。それが天才への第一歩。

3: In 2038, the world could be applauding your child's second Nobel Prize! Every Nobel Prize winner was a child once. Choose intelligent toys and get your kid's future off a good start. Plan to build a genius.
2038年。お子さんの2回目のノーベル賞受賞に世界が喝采を贈っているかも。ノーベル賞の受賞者も、昔はみんな子ども。知能を育てる玩具を選んで、未来へのスタートを切る。それが天才への第一歩。

Plan Creations
Toy Manufacturer
玩具メーカー
Thailand 1997
CD, CW: Anurux Jansanjai
AD, D: Thirasak Tanapatanakul
P: Somporn Chotigo
I: Anuchai Secharunputong
A: Ogilvy & Mather

Nike Europe
Sports Apparel Maker
スポーツ用品メーカー
Netherlands 1997
CD, CW: Johan Kramer
CD, AD, D: Erik Kessels
I: Bill Mayer
CW: Tyler Whisnand
DF: Kesselskramer

LET **AIRPLANES** GET CAUGHT IN YOUR **HAIR**

TEAM UP! Europe's first outdoor 5 on 5 basketball tour WATERSPORTBAAN GENT 28 & 29 JUNI 1997 HOTLINE informatienummer: 09 2254850

Summer Hoops '97

GIVE **NAMES** TO ALL THE **CLOUDS**

TEAM UP! Europe's first outdoor 5 on 5 basketball tour JAARBEURSCOMPLEX UTRECHT 5 & 6 JULI 1997 HOTLINE informatienummer: 0165 570271

Summer Hoops '97

HANG OUT IN THE **IONOSPHERE**

TEAM UP! Europe's first outdoor 5 on 5 basketball tour JAARBEURSCOMPLEX UTRECHT 5 & 6 JULI 1997 HOTLINE informatienummer: 0165 570271

Summer Hoops '97

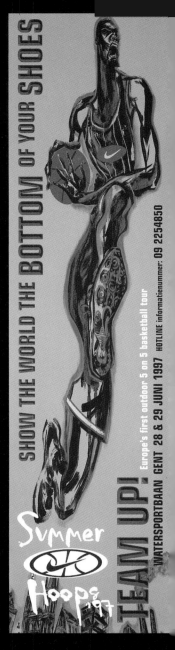

SHOW THE WORLD THE **BOTTOM** OF YOUR **SHOES**

TEAM UP! Europe's first outdoor 5 on 5 basketball tour WATERSPORTBAAN GENT 28 & 29 JUNI 1997 HOTLINE informatienummer: 09 2254850

Summer Hoops '97

Hoofdbedrijfschap Ambachten-Schoonheidsspecialisten
Beauticians Association
エステティシャン協会
Netherlands 1997-98
CD, AD: Erik Kruize
D: Zware Jongens
P: Jerome Esch
CW: Massimo van der Plas
A: FCA!

You can't go on like this. You're at the age when your body and mind should be in top condition. Go discover your true face. With even a short treatment, miracles will happen.
あんた、このままじゃだめ。今こそ身体と心を磨く時。自分の本当の顔を創りだすのよ。ちょっとやってもらうだけで奇跡が起きる、必ず。

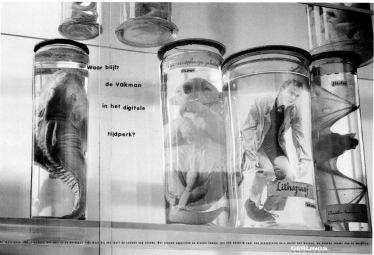

Gerlings
Pre - Press Services
版下制作会社
Netherlands 1995
CD: Jeroen van Zwam / Marcel Hartog
P: Ernst Yperlaan
Paintbox: Willem Heuvelmans
A: Result DDB

What's going to happen to those with skills in the digital age?
デジタル化時代には、熟練した職人たちはどうなるか。
1: Retoucher =修整職人
2: Micro monteur = 精密組み立て職人
3: Lithograaf = リトグラフ職人

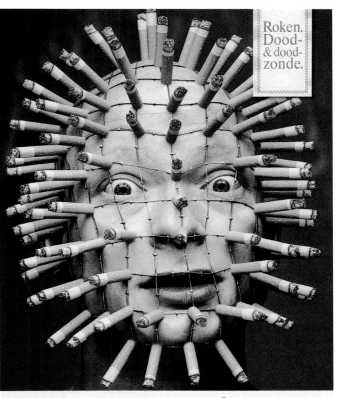

Stichting Volksgezondheid en Roken
Anti-Smoking Organization
嫌煙家協会
Netherlands 1997
AD: Ron Gessel
P: Gerdjan van de Lugt
CW: Erik Jousma
DF: BvH

Arkaden
Shopping Center
ショッピングセンター
Norway 1997
AD: Anne Gravingen
P: Per Heimly
CW: Benoik Romstad
A: Bates Camp

Young people nowdays / 今の若者たち

SOME SEE SENIOR CITIZENS. WE SEE A BOOM IN CONDO CONSTRUCTION, NEW BUSINESS START-UPS AND INCREASED DEMAND FOR THE GOLF CHANNEL.

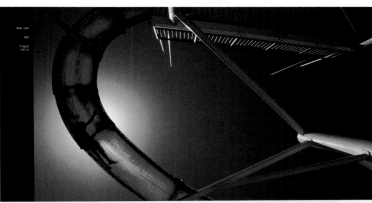

FORGET THE CORKSCREW ROLLER COASTER AND THE CENTRIFUGE RIDE. NOTHING TAKES YOUR BREATH AWAY LIKE LOSING A MULTIMILLION-DOLLAR LAWSUIT.

WITHOUT THE RIGHT COVERAGE, YOUR COMPANY CAN BE FLATTENED BY A TRAIN THAT'S STANDING STILL.

DUMP THEM, YOU BREAK THE LAW. RECYCLE IMPROPERLY, YOU BREAK THE LAW. MEANWHILE, MORE TIRES JUST CAME IN.

1 2
3 4

1: Some see senior citizens. We see a boom in condo construction, new business start-ups and increased demand for the golf channel.
ある人は高齢者しかみない。私たちには見えます。マンション建設ブーム。ニュービジネス。そしてゴルフ番組が増えるでしょう。
2: Forget the corkscrew roller coaster and the centrifuge ride. Nothing takes your breath away like losing a multimillion-dollar lawsuit.
コークスクリューも絶叫マシンも忘れなさい。数百万ドルの裁判に負けるほうがよっぽど寒気がします。
3: Without the right coverage, your company can be flattened by a train that's standing still.
きちんと保険をかけないと、あなたの会社は止まったままの電車に轢かれてぺっちゃんこ。
4: Dump them, you break the law. Recycle improperly, you break the law. Meanwhile, more tires just came in.
投げ捨て。それは法律違反。間違ったリサイクル。それも法律違反。ほら、またタイヤが来ました。

AIG Financial Services
Insurance and Financial Services
保険会社
USA 1997
CD: Mark Ledermann
CD, AD, D: Steve Juliusson
P: David Hurn (1) / Arch Chevey (2)
/ Alex Maclean (3) / José Azul (4)
CW: Robin Landis
A: Ogilvy & Mather Advertising (New York)

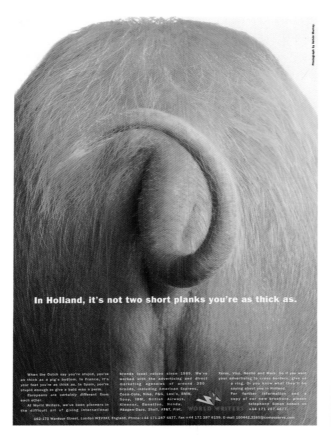

World Writers
Advertisement Adaptations for International Markets
広告翻案会社
UK 1996
CD: John Hegarty
AD: Jamie Colona
P: Kelvin Murray
CW: James Betts
A: Bartle Bogle Hegarty Ltd.

1: In Holland, It's not two short planks you're as thick as.
オランダでは、「板切れ二枚の厚みしかない as thick as two short planks」からといって「まぬけ」ではありません。
2: In France, it isn't the gas a driver steps on.
フランスでは、「ガソリンを踏む step on the gas」からといって「スピードを上げる」わけではありません。
3: In Italy, It doesn't rain cats and dogs.
イタリアでは、「猫と犬に降る rain cats and dogs」からといって「どしゃ降りの雨」ではありません。
4: In Germany, no one bites the dust.
ドイツでは、「土を噛む bite the dust」からといって「負け」ではありません。

index

SUBMITTOR INDEX

CLIENT INDEX

Magazine Advertising Graphics
マガジン　アドバタイジング　グラフィックス

Art Director & Designer: Kazuo Abe
Editor: Kaoru Yamashita
Photographer: Seiichi Kazunaga+Sook Studio
Translators: Douglas Allsopp, Setsuko Noguchi, ID Corp.
Typesetter: Yutaka Hasegawa
Publisher: Shingo Miyoshi

1998年9月19日初版第1刷発行

発行所　ピエ・ブックス
〒170-0003　東京都豊島区駒込4-14-6-301
編集　TEL: 03-3949-5010　FAX: 03-3949-5650
営業　TEL: 03-3940-8302　FAX: 03-3576-7361
e-mail: piebooks@bekkoame.ne.jp

©1998 by P・I・E BOOKS

ISBN4-89444-082-2

Printed in Japan

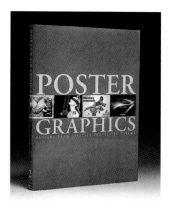

POSTER GRAPHICS Vol. 2
好評！業種別世界のポスター集大成、第2弾
Pages: 256 (192 in color) ￥16,505＋Tax
700 posters from the top creators in Japan and abroad are showcased in this book - classified by business. This invaluable reference makes it easy to compare design trends among various industries and corporations.

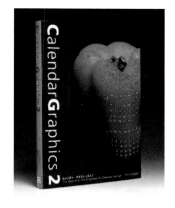

CALENDAR GRAPHICS Vol. 2
好評カレンダー・デザイン集の決定版、第2弾
Pages: 224 (192 in Color) ￥15,534＋Tax
The second volume of our popular "Calendar Graphics" series features designs from about 250 1994 and 1995 calendars from around the world. A special collection that includes mass market as well as exclusive corporate PR calendars.

BROCHURE & PAMPHLET COLLECTION Vol. 4
好評！業種別カタログ・コレクション、第4弾
Pages: 224 (Full Color) ￥15,534＋Tax
The fourth volume in our popular "Brochure & Pamphlet" series. Twelve types of businesses are represented through artwork that really sells. This book conveys a sense of what's happening right now in the catalog design scene. A must for all creators.

BROCHURE DESIGN FORUM Vol. 3
世界の最新カタログ・コレクション、第3弾
Pages: 224 (Full Color) ￥15,534＋Tax
A special edition of our "Brochure & Pamphlet Collection" featuring 250 choice pieces that represent 70 types of businesses and are classified by business for handy reference. A compendium of the design scene at a glance.

COMPANY BROCHURE COLLECTION
業種別（会社・学校・施設）案内グラフィックス
Pages: 224 (192 in Color) ￥15,534＋Tax
A special selection of brochures and catalogs ranging from admission manuals for colleges and universities, to amusement facility and hotel guidebooks, to corporate and organization profiles. The entries are classified by industry for easy reference.

COMPANY BROCHURE COLLECTION Vol. 2
業種別会社案内グラフィックス、第2弾！
Pages: 224 (Full Color) ￥15,534＋Tax
Showing imaginative layouts that present information clearly in a limited space, and design that effectively enhances corporate identity, this volume will prove to be an essential source book for graphic design work of the future.

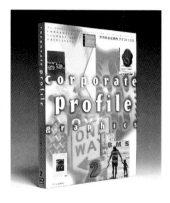

CORPORATE PROFILE GRAPHICS Vol. 2
世界の会社案内グラフィックス、第2弾
Pages: 224 (Full Color) ￥15,534＋Tax
An extensive collection of company brochures, annual reports, school facility guides and organization pamphlets. Brochures are fully detailed from cover to inner pages, illustrating clearly the importance of cohesiveness and flow. An essential catalog design reference volume.

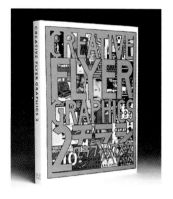

CREATIVE FLYER GRAPHICS Vol. 2
世界のフライヤーデザイン傑作集
Pages: 224 (Full Color) ￥15,534＋Tax
A pack of some 600 flyers and leaflets incorporating information from a variety of events including exhibitions, movies, plays, concerts, live entertainment and club events, as well as foods, cosmetics, electrical merchandise and travel packages.

EVENT FLYER GRAPHICS
世界のイベントフライヤー・コレクション
Pages: 224 (Full Color) ￥15,534＋Tax
Here's a special selection focusing on flyers promoting events. This upbeat selection covers a wide range of music events, as well as movies, exhibitions and the performing arts.

ADVERTISING FLYER GRAPHICS
衣・食・住・遊の商品チラシ特集
Pages: 224 (Full Color) ￥15,534＋Tax
The eye-catching flyers selected for this new collection represent a broad spectrum of businesses, and are presented in a loose classification covering four essential modern lifestyle themes: fashion, dining, home and leisure.

TRAVEL & LEISURE GRAPHICS
ホテル＆旅行案内グラフィックス
Pages: 224 (Full Color) ￥15,534＋Tax
A giant collection of some 400 pamphlets, posters and direct mailings exclusively created for hotels, inns, resort tours and amusement facilities.

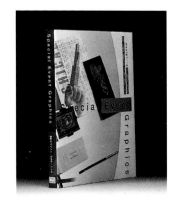

SPECIAL EVENT GRAPHICS
世界のイベント・グラフィックス
Pages: 224 (192 in Color) ￥15,534＋Tax
A showcase for event graphics, introducing leaflets for exhibitions, fashion shows, all sorts of sales promotional campaigns, posters, premiums and actual installation scenes from events around the world. An invaluable and inspirational resource book, unique in the world of graphic publishing.

THE P·I·E COLLECTION

1, 2 & 3 COLOR GRAPHICS Vol. 2
1・2・3色グラフィックス、第2弾
Pages: 224 (Full Color) ¥15,534＋Tax
Even more ambitious in scale than the first volume, this second collection of graphics displays the unique talents of graphic designers who work with limited colors. An essential reference guide to effective, low-cost designing.

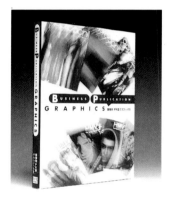

BUSINESS PUBLICATION GRAPHICS
業種別企業PR誌・フリーペーパーの集大成！
Pages: 224 (Full Color) ¥15,534＋Tax
This comprehensive graphic book introduces business publications created for a variety of business needs, including promotions from boutiques and department stores, exclusive clubs, local communities, and company newsletters.

SHOPPING BAG GRAPHICS
世界の最新ショッピングバッグ・デザイン集
Pages: 224 (Full Color) ¥15,534＋Tax
Over 500 samples of the latest and best of the world's shopping bag designs from a wide range of retail businesses! This volume features a selection of shopping bags originating in Tokyo, NY, LA, London, Paris, Milan, and other major cities worldwide, presented here in a useful business classification.

1 & 2 COLOR GRAPHICS
1色＆2色デザインの大特集
Pages: 224 (Full Color) ¥15,534＋Tax
Powerful design achieved by restricting colors, unusual combinations of colors that grab the attention, enhanced stylishness of script... all artwork featured in this worldwide collection makes a dramatic visual impact. A useful book, too, for exploring the possibilities of low-cost design.

BUSINESS PUBLICATION GRAPHICS Vol. 2
大好評！業種別PR誌の集大成、第2弾
Pages: 224 (Full Color) ¥15,534＋Tax
One volume offering more than 150 samples of regularly published PR and other informative magazines, covering different business sectors from fashion labels to non-profit organizations. This overviews the current trends in PR magazine design aimed at attracting the attention of a specific readership in commercial activities.

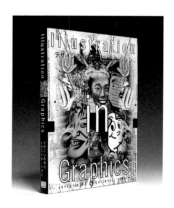

ILLUSTRATION IN GRAPHICS
イラストレーションを使った広告特集
Pages: 224 (Full Color) ¥15,534＋Tax
Delivering the message faster than photos and more accurately than words, illustration never fails to stir the imagination. This superb selection presents some 600 first-class illustrations for advertising from across the business spectrum and for editorial designs.

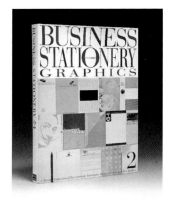

BUSINESS STATIONERY GRAPHICS Vol. 2
世界のレターヘッド・コレクション、第2弾
Pages: 224 (172 in Color) ¥15,534＋Tax
The second volume in our popular 'Business Stationery Graphics' series. This publication focuses on letterheads, envelopes and business cards, all classified by business. This collection will serve artists and business people well.

POSTCARD GRAPHICS Vol. 4
世界の業種別ポストカード・コレクション
Pages: 224 (192 in Color) ¥15,534＋Tax
Our popular "Postcard Graphics" series has been revamped for "Postcard Graphics Vol. 4." This first volume of the new version showcases approximately 1,000 pieces ranging from direct mailers to private greeting cards, selected from the best around the world.

PRESENTATION GRAPHICS
制作の現場 プレゼンテーション・グラフィックス
Pages: 224 (Full Color) ¥15,500＋Tax
31 designers from 8 countries explain the production side of the creative process. Here are idea sketches, comps, presentations, and final works, all with explanatory notes by the designer. This is a unique volume that peeks behind the scenes of the creator's world.

NEW BUSINESS CARD GRAPHICS
最新版！ビジネスカード・グラフィックス
Pages: 224 (Full Color) ¥15,534＋Tax
A selection of 900 samples representing the works of top designers worldwide. Covering the broadest spectrum of business cards, it ranges from the trendiest to the most classy and includes highly original examples along the way.

SEASONAL CAMPAIGN GRAPHICS
デパート・ショップのキャンペーン広告特集
Pages: 224 (Full Color) ¥15,534＋Tax
A spirited collection of quality graphics for sales campaigns planned around the four seasons, Christmas, St. Valentine's Day and the Japanese gift-giving seasons, as well as for store openings, anniversaries, and similar events.

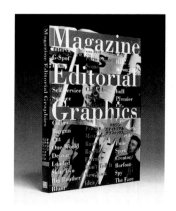

MAGAZINE EDITORIAL GRAPHICS
世界のエディトリアル＆カバーデザイン特集
Pages: 224 (Full Color) ¥15,500＋Tax
A special collection of editorial and cover designs. Stylish and sophisticated, 79 topical books from 9 countries were selected. Including top creators graphic works, innovative fashion photography, and the latest typography. this is a true creator's bible for the New Age.

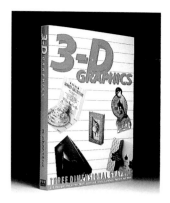

3-D GRAPHICS
3Dグラフィックスの大百科
Pages: 224 (192 in Color) ¥15,534＋Tax
350 works that demonstrate some of the finest examples of 3-D graphic methods, including DMs, catalogs, posters, POPs and more. The volume is a virtual encyclopedia of 3-D graphics.

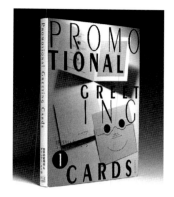

PROMOTIONAL GREETING CARDS
ADVERTISING GREETING CARDS Vol. 4
（English Title）
世界の案内状＆ダイレクトメール集大成．
Pages: 224 (Full Color) ¥15,534＋Tax
A total of 500 examples of cards from designers around the world. A whole spectrum of stylish and inspirational cards, classified by function for easy reference.

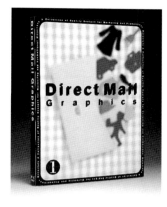

DIRECT MAIL GRAPHICS Vol. 1
衣・食・住のセールスＤＭ特集
Pages: 224 (Full Color) ¥15,534＋Tax
The long-awaited design collection featuring direct mailers that have outstanding sales impact and quality design. 350 of the best pieces, classified into 100 business categories. A veritable textbook of current direct marketing design.

DIRECT MAIL GRAPHICS Vol. 2
好評！衣・食・住のセールスＤＭ特集！第２弾
Pages: 224 (Full Color) ¥15,534＋Tax
The second volume in our extremely popular "Direct Mail Graphics" series features a whole range of direct mailers for various purposes; from commercial announcements to seasonal greetings. Classfied by industry.

SUCCESSFUL DIRECT MAIL DESIGN
セールス効果の高いDMデザイン集！
Pages: 224 (Full Color) ¥15,500＋Tax
This collection features product flyers, service guides, shop opening and sale announcements, school and industrial promotions, and a variety of event invitations. A valuable book that captures the essence of today's direct marketing design.

The Paris Collections / INVITATION CARDS
パリ・コレクションの招待状グラフィックス
Pages: 176 (Full Color) ¥13,396＋Tax
This book features 400 announcements for and invitations to the Paris Collections, produced by the world's top names in fashion over the past 10 years. A treasure trove of ideas and pure fun to browse through.

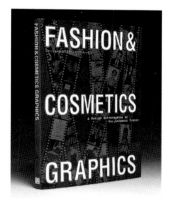

FASHION & COSMETICS GRAPHICS
ファッション＆コスメティック・グラフィックス
Pages: 208 (Full Color) ¥15,534＋Tax
A collection of promotional graphics from around the world produced for apparel, accessory and cosmetic brands at the avantgarde of the fashion industry. 40 brands featured in this book point the way toward future trends in advertising.

THE TOKYO TYPEDIRECTORS CLUB ANNUAL 1995-96
TDC 年鑑95-96
Pages: 250 (Full Color) ¥16,505＋Tax
A follow-up publication to Japan's only international graphic deisgn competition. Featuring 650 typographic artworks selected by THE TOKYO TYPEDIRECTORS CLUB, this book provides a window to the latest typographic design concepts worldwide.

The Production Index ARTIFILE Vol. 5
最新版プロダクション・クリエーター年鑑
Pages: 224 (Full Color) ¥12,136＋Tax
ARTIFILE 5 features artwork from a total of 100 top Japanese production companies and designers, along with company data and messages from the creators. An invaluable information source for anyone who needs to keep up with the latest developments in the graphic scene.

CARTOON CHARACTER COLLECTION
5500種のキャラクターデザイン大百科
Pages: 480 (B&W) ¥3,600＋Tax
A collection of illustrations from successful character artists. People, animals, plants, food, vehicles, landscapes, sports, seasons... Nearly 5,500 works are presented, conveniently categorized. A collection full of ideas sure to come in handy when designing greeting cards and illustrations.

CATALOGUE AND PAMPHLET COLLECTION
/ Soft Jacket
業種別商品カタログ特集／ソフトカバー
Pages: 224 (Full Color) ¥3,689＋Tax
A collection of the world's most outstanding brochures, catalogs and leaflets classified by industry such as fashion, restaurants, music, interiors and sporting goods. Presenting each piece in detail from cover to inside pages. This title is an indispensable sourcebook for all graphic designers and CI professionals.

SPORTS GRAPHICS / Soft Jacket
世界のスポーツグッズ・コレクション
／ソフトカバー
Pages: 224 (192 in Color) ¥3,689＋Tax
A Collection of 1,000 bold sporting goods graphic works from all over the world. A wide variety of goods are shown, including uniforms, bags, shoes and other gear. Covers all sorts of sports: basketball, skiing, surfing, and many, many more.

**LABELS AND TAGS COLLECTION Vol. 1
/ Soft Jacket**
ラベル＆タグ・コレクション／ソフトカバー
Pages: 224 (192 in Color) ￥3,689＋Tax
Nowhere is brand recognition more important
than in Japan. Here is a collection of 1,600
labels and tags from Japan's 450 top fashion
names with page after page of women's and
men's clothing and sportswear designs.

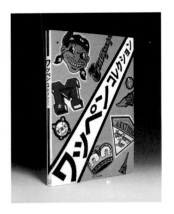

**FASHION INSIGNIA COLLECTION
/ Soft Jacket**
ワッペン・コレクション／ソフトカバー
Pages: 224 (Full Color) ￥3,689＋Tax
Over 300 designs were scrutinized for this
collection of 1000 outstanding emblems and
embroidered motifs. Visually exciting, they
make innovative use of materials and
compliment the fashions with which they are
worn.

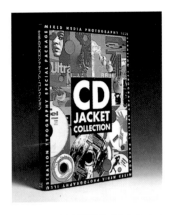

CD JACKET COLLECTION / Soft Jacket
世界のCDジャケット・コレクション
／ソフトカバー
Pages: 224 (192 in Color) ￥3,689＋Tax
Featuring 700 of the world's most imaginative
CD and LP covers from all musical genres,
this is a must-have book for all design and
music professionals.

POSTCARD COLLECTION Vol. 2 / Soft Jacket
好評 ポストカード・コレクション、第２弾
／ソフトカバー
Pages: 230 (Full Color) ￥3,689＋Tax
Welcome to the colorful world of postcards,
with 1200 postcards created by artists from
all over the world classified according to the
business of the client.

POSTCARD COLLECTION / Soft Jacket
世界のポストカード・コレクション
／ソフトカバー
Pages: 240 (Full Color) ￥3,689＋Tax
Postcards from top Japanese designers,
fashion brands, and famous shops. This
book shows how designers, using beautiful
photos and fun illustrations, pack a lot of
creativity into a postcard's limited space.

DIAGRAM COLLECTION
世界のダイアグラム・デザイン集大成
Pages: 224 (192 in Color) ￥3,700＋Tax
Graphs, charts, maps, architectural diagrams
and plans, product and scientific illustrations.
Almost 400 diagrams selected from designs
sent to us by some of the world's most
talented creators. This invaluable volume
shows the many possibilities of diagram
design.

WORLD BUSINESS CARD COLLECTION
世界の名刺コレクション Vol. 2
Pages: 224 (192 in Color) ￥3,700＋Tax
From personal and business cards, bursting
with individuality, to colorfully creative shop
cards, we introduce nearly 1,000 of the best.
Limited in size, these designs mix fun and
cleverness, and will impress and delight you
with their originality.

カタログ・新刊のご案内について
総合カタログ、新刊案内をご希望の方は、はさみ込みのアンケートはがきを
ご返送いただくか、90円切手同封の上、ピエ・ブックス宛お申し込み下さい。

**CATALOGUES ET INFORMATIONS SUR LES NOUVELLES
PUBLICATIONS**
Si vous désirez recevoir un exemplaire gratuit de notre catalogue général
ou des détails sur nos nouvelles publications, veuillez compléter la carte
réponse incluse et nous la retourner par courrierou par fax.

CATALOGS and INFORMATION ON NEW PUBLICATIONS
If you would like to receive a free copy of our general catalog or
details of our new publications, please fill out the enclosed postcard
and return it to us by mail or fax.

CATALOGE und INFORMATIONEN ÜBER NEUE TITLE
Wenn Sie unseren Gesamtkatalog oder Detailinformationen über
unsere neuen Titel wünschen, fullen Sie bitte die beigefügte Postkarte
aus und schicken Sie sie uns per Post oder Fax.

ピエ・ブックス
〒170 東京都豊島区駒込 4-14-6-301
TEL: 03-3940-8302 FAX: 03-3576-7361

P·I·E BOOKS
#301, 4-14-6, Komagome, Toshima-ku, Tokyo 170 JAPAN
TEL: 03-3940-8302 FAX: 03-3576-7361

	17-7-01
	✓
	✓
...ne	✓
...ver	✓
memo	
barcode	R62824
...al check	